JUMPST
MUSIC

Children develop their musicality best through engaging and partici-pating, and an effective and enriching music curriculum must focus on the development of practical music-making skills. *Jumpstart! Music* therefore contains a wealth of ideas and activities that will support any teacher as they aid the musical learning of pupils aged 7 to 14, helping students not only to learn in new and exciting ways, but also to enjoy themselves while they are doing it.

Inspiring any young learner to listen to, make and create a range of music, the book includes multiple simple-to-use ideas and activities, with every chapter based around fun and engaging topics, such as:

- Storytelling
- History
- Media
- Modern music
- Technology
- The world

With group suggestions as well as opportunities for the students to develop their skills independently, the games and ideas featured in this title all focus on the core skills in learning music – listening, singing, playing, improvising, composing and SMSC (spiritual, moral, social, cul-tural) – and are all flexible enough to be adapted to fit each individual situation, whatever the resources to hand.

Jumpstart! Music is an essential classroom resource for helping young learners develop their musicality and musicianship and will support any teacher in delivering engaging, inclusive and creative music lessons.

Kelly-Jo Foster-Peters has been teaching curriculum music in schools for 20 years in both mainstream and SEND schools. She is the SEND music teacher representative on the DfE Music Hubs Advisory Board, and the SEND music advisor for Southampton Music Hub.

Jumpstart!

Jumpstart! Wellbeing
Games and Activities for Ages 7–14
Steve Bowkett and Kevin Hogston

Jumpstart! Study Skills
Games and Activities for Active Learning, Ages 7–12
John Foster

Jumpstart! Philosophy in the Classroom
Games & Activities for Ages 7–14
Steve Bowkett

Jumpstart! RE
Games and Activities for Ages 7–12
Imran Mogra

Jumpstart! Creativity (2nd Edition)
Games & Activities for Ages 7–14
Steve Bowkett

Jumpstart! Drama (2nd Edition)
Games and Activities for Ages 5–11
Teresa Cremin, Roger McDonald, Emma Longley and Louise Blakemore

Jumpstart! Assemblies
Ideas and Activities For Assemblies in Primary Schools
John Foster

Jumpstart! Maths (3rd Edition)
Maths Activities and Games for Ages 5–14
John Taylor

Jumpstart! Music
Ideas and Activities for Ages 7–14
Kelly-Jo Foster-Peters

For a full list of titles in this series visit
www.routledge.com/Jumpstart/book-series/JUMP

JUMPSTART!
MUSIC

IDEAS AND ACTIVITIES FOR AGES 7–14

Kelly-Jo Foster-Peters

Routledge
Taylor & Francis Group

LONDON AND NEW YORK

First published 2020
by Routledge
2 Park Square, Milton Park, Abingdon, Oxon OX14 4RN

and by Routledge
52 Vanderbilt Avenue, New York, NY 10017

Routledge is an imprint of the Taylor & Francis Group, an informa business

British Library Cataloguing-in-Publication Data
A catalogue record for this book is available from the British Library

Library of Congress Cataloging-in-Publication Data
Names: Foster-Peters, Kelly-Jo, author.
Title: Jumpstart! music: ideas and activities for ages 7–14 /
Kelly-Jo Foster-Peters.
Description: New York : Routledge, 2020. |
Identifiers: LCCN 2019053962 (print) | LCCN 2019053963 (ebook) |
ISBN 9780367263270 (hardback) | ISBN 9780367263287 (paperback) |
ISBN 9780429292613 (ebook)
Subjects: LCSH: School music–Instruction and study–Activity programs.
Classification: LCC MT10 .F79 2020 (print) |
LCC MT10 (ebook) | DDC 372.87/044–dc23
LC record available at https://lccn.loc.gov/2019053962
LC ebook record available at https://lccn.loc.gov/2019053963

ISBN: 978-0-367-26327-0 (hbk)
ISBN: 978-0-367-26328-7 (pbk)
ISBN: 978-0-429-29261-3 (ebk)

Typeset in Palatino & Scala Sans
by Newgen Publishing UK
Printed and bound by CPI Group (UK) Ltd, Croydon CR0 4YY

Contents

Contents

Acknowledgements

Thank you to my parents Angela and Roger Hardy for their support and encouragement.

Introduction

Many decades ago music education in school consisted of sitting at a desk and writing western classical notation. Through the years the emphasis on learning notation in schools has shifted. Now an effective and enriching music curriculum focuses more on the development of practical music-making skills. Music teachers typically use a variety of fun activities to support their pupils' musical development. This is important because children ought to be looking forward to an engaging and interactive music lesson instead of the expectation of sitting at a desk with pen and paper. Music learning needs to be enjoyable and offer pupils an opportunity to learn in a different way to other subjects, thereby contributing to the education of the whole child. Through interacting with music learning in these ways, pupils become more engaged and look forward to their music lessons. Thus, they make better progress and achieve more.

This book covers a variety of topics and suggests a range of musical ideas and activities for each topic. The overall sense of musical progression should focus on skill development. Therefore, each topic selected enables teachers to support their pupils in building on previously learnt skills. In teaching the music curriculum it is widely recognised that the development of musical abilities increases primarily through the following skill set:

- Listening (critical engagement)
- Singing
- Playing
- Improvising
- Composing
- SMSC (spiritual, moral, social, cultural)

The improvement of listening and aural skills is fundamental to the process of developing a person's musicality. Therefore, the ability to listen critically, with full attention, concentration and engagement is optimum for learning.

Singing is easily accessible to everyone and is free in cost. YouTube has made singing widely accessible and offers both karaoke and instrumental backings for most songs, old and new. Accompanying children on acoustic instruments such as piano or guitar is ideal. This is a skill to be encouraged among all music teachers. Again, YouTube offers many tutorials.

Music teaching should give opportunities for the students to develop their skills working independently, and importantly with others too, whether in pairs, small groups or whole classes. The ideas and activities suggest opportunities for teachers to support their pupils to play, improvise and compose music using a variety of methods, supporting both solo and ensemble skills. Every music department has access to different instruments and technology. Therefore, most activities are flexible enough to be adapted to fit each individual situation. Each classroom will have a different set of resources, whether it be keyboards, tuned or untuned percussion, or other instruments. There may be no instruments at all. Therefore, alternative options for many activities are to use the voice and body percussion, or create sound using everyday items and junk percussion.

Composing starts with the exploration of sound, building up to the creation of a small musical idea, whether a few chosen notes or rhythms, then to structuring a piece of music of length. It is very popular to use technology today as it offers young people a wide array of sounds and the ability to compose music without the need for being able to play an instrument. This focuses solely on the ability to combine sounds effectively together. The composing activities in this book combine different ideas for composing with and without technology, though most ideas can be adapted to fit either pedagogy.

In this book, the activities include opportunities for supporting young learners in their spiritual, moral, social, and cultural development. This is fully embedded throughout the topics. The music teacher's role works differently to other subjects. In order to offer as full and enriching SMSC curriculum as possible, a music teacher should utilise the support of others. Whether this support includes teachers in the school to help run concerts, peripatetic teachers teaching instrumental lessons, performance opportunities and visiting artists organised by the music hub. Children are inspired by the world around them and so any opportunity to help them see a live performance is essential.

CHAPTERS

Chapter 1 Music and the environment

Music and the environment is a great starting point to learn about the elements of music through its focus on characterisation. Whether portraying the different characteristics of animals, planets, or moods and atmospheres created at sea or in space. There are many ideas and creative approaches for engaging children in musical learning.

Chapter 2 Music and storytelling

The skill of telling a story through music or being able to access somebody else's story requires a deeper understanding of how music works. This chapter supports teachers by giving an insight into how to help pupils learn these methods of musical expression and how the music elements can be further understood to compose structured pieces of music.

Chapter 3 Music and history

Learning about music in its historical context gives an insight into how music has developed through time. The role of music in society has helped to shape both creative and political thinking. This chapter has ideas and activities to help teachers support young people gain knowledge and understanding about the impact music has had, and continues to have, in our ever-evolving world.

Chapter 4 Music and events
Music and events builds on the knowledge that music is involved in many different types of events and celebrations in a variety of cultures. This chapter covers a range of sporting, celebration and religious events, with a focus on Christmas music.

Chapter 5 Music and media
Music and media connects different aspects of young peoples' worlds with music learning in school. Developing thinking skills to discover how music affects us through the TV (animations and films) we watch, the adverts we see, or the computer games we play.

Chapter 6 Modern music
Modern music traces the development of music starting from where the blues influences both jazz, and rock and roll styles in the early 20th century. It breaks down a history of modern music by decades and gives insight into the music pupils listen to in modern times.

Chapter 7 Music and technology
Technological developments have been integral to the exploration and advancement of music styles and music education. This chapter predominantly gives insight to teachers on how youth culture interacts with music and how to link their music learning outside of school, to their music learning inside of school.

Chapter 8 Music from around the globe
Learning about how globalisation and music affects the cultural, historical, and political advancement of communities in different countries is important for the development of pupils into whole-rounded global citizens. This chapter showcases a variety of music from different cultures, enabling teachers to use within their curriculum teaching.

CHAPTER 1

Music and the environment

1.1 ANIMALS

Animals works well as a stand-alone topic in primary school, or in year 7 at secondary school. It can be incorporated into related topics such as *The Jungle, Habitats, Dinosaurs* or linked to science topics about minibeasts or animal biology. There are many resources aimed at a range of abilities, encompassing all music skill areas.

1.1.1 Listening activities

Make a set of elements of music prompt cards, write some elements on the white board, or write general listening questions on a PowerPoint as a resource to use each time you do a listening activity. The aim is to get children to do more focused listening in order to develop their aural skills.

Element of music:	Description:
Pitch	High/low
Tempo	Speed – fast/slow
Dynamics	Volume – soft/loud
Timbre	Type of sound/instrument
Attack and decay	Start and end of a note
Duration	Length of the note, section or piece
Texture	Number of parts/layers
Structure	Building blocks/sections of the piece

Activity 1: *The Carnival of the Animals* (Camille Saint-Saens, 1886)

The Carnival of the Animals is a suite of 14 light-hearted short pieces of classical music. Each piece represents a different animal and the music caricatures the features of the animal. Play each piece in class and ask pupils to guess which animal they can hear. Ask them why they have selected each animal so that a discussion can be had on how the musical elements have been used to characterise the features of the animal. There are many resources online that have teaching materials associated with this piece:

- **Swan** – Slow, graceful, quiet, tuneful, melodic, long notes, a cello plays a gliding melody over a piano accompaniment that represents the rippling water.
- **Lion** – March, proud, confident, loud, kingly, the piano uses the full pitch range to glide over the piano keys and produce a sound similar to a roar.
- **Kangaroo** – jumpy, up and down, grace notes, using the full range of the pitch and octaves on a piano.
- **Aquarium** – Shimmering, high piano notes twinkling, sparkling, makes you think of the light glistening on the ocean with shoals of silver fish swimming in the light.
- **The cuckoo** – a clarinet makes the 'cuckoo sound' over a piano accompaniment/backing.
- **The tortoise** – Saint-Saens has fun here and plays the normally lively French *Can-Can* at a tremendously slow speed, painfully slow almost, giving the piece an element of irony and fun.
- **Fossils** – Interesting that fossils have a place in the Carnival of 'Animals'; however, the result is a delightful xylophone solo, giving the bony effect if you were to imagine playing a set of bones. This song is very well known and has been used in adverts. Spot the 'Twinkle Twinkle' tune in the middle of the piece.

Other pieces in the suite are titled: *Hens and roosters* (pecking sounds); *Aviary* (flutes twittering like birds); *Wild donkeys and swift animals*; *Characters with long ears* (Eeyore sounds on the violin).

Activity 2: *Peter and the Wolf* (Sergei Prokofiev, 1936)

Peter and the Wolf is an orchestral piece by the Russian composer Prokofiev. It lasts approximately 15 minutes and is often accompanied by a narration or animation. Each character in the story is represented by a different instrument and so it is a great way to introduce young people to the following instruments:

Violins	Peter
Flute	Bird
Clarinet	Cat
Oboe	Duck
Bassoon	Grandfather
Horns	Wolf
Drums	Hunters

Watch an animation (see YouTube link below) and have a competition to see who puts their hand up each time they hear a different instrument being played. Ask pupils why they think the sound of each particular instrument suits the character it represents.

Peter and the Wolf animation:

YouTube – *Pierre et le Loup Suzie Templeton 2009*, posted by csm p6b [19 Jan. 2016] https://youtu.be/Z5ppQw1SNFw

Further listening
- *Fantastic Beasts and Where to Find Them* (James Newton Howard, London: WaterTower Music, 2016)
- *Animals* (Pink Floyd, 1977)
- *Catalogue d'oiseaux* (Olivier Messiaen, 1958)
- *The Birds* (Ottorino Respighi, 1928)

The *BBC Ten Pieces* website www.bbc.co.uk/teach/ten-pieces contains teaching resources for the following pieces of music linked to animals:

- *Anthology of Fantastic Zoology*: *Sprite and A Bao A Qu* (Mason Bates, 2015). The piece lasts approximately 30 minutes long and is separated into 11 shorter movements, each representing a different mythical creature.
- *The Lark Ascending* (Ralph Vaughan-Williams, 1914)
- *The Firebird Suite* (Igor Stravinsky, 1911)

1.1.2 Singing
Vocal warm-ups
Get pupils to warm-up their voices by copying the following animal sounds:

- Ooh ah, ooh, ah, hee, hee, heeeee (monkey)
- Snap, snap, snap, snap, roll, roll, crunch (crocodile)
- Miaow, miaow, purr (cat)

Pupils can make up their own animal sounds, and actions.

Suggested songs
There are lots of songs from a variety of genre that are associated with animals that can be used as inspiration for developing singing skills. Different versions of all songs can be found on YouTube.

Children's songs:
- o 'The Ants Go Marching' (Into the Ark)
- o 'The Animals Went in Two by Two' (Into the Ark)
- o ''The Hippopotamus Song: A Muddy Love Story' (Flanders and Swann, 1957)
- o 'Alice the Camel' (trad.)

Songs from musicals:
- o *The Jungle Book* (1967)
- o *Cats* (1981)
- o *The Lion King* (1994)

Pop songs:
- o 'How Much Is That Doggy in the Window?' (Patti Page, 1953)
- o 'The Lion Sleeps Tonight' (The Tokens, RCA Victor, 1961)
- o 'The Eye of the Tiger' (Survivor, EMI, 1982)
- o 'Roar' (Katy Perry, 2013)
- o 'Baby Shark' (Pingfong, 2016)

1.1.3 Playing
Playing keyboard instruments or tuned percussion

In music, all music keyboards (piano, synthesiser etc.) have 7 white notes and 5 black notes, making 12 notes in total. The white notes each have a letter name, A to G. The black notes are used when a white note is flattened/lowered by one pitch or sharpened/raised by one pitch. The symbol for playing the black note to the left (lower in sound) is a flat – b. The symbol for playing the black note to the right (higher in sound) is a sharp – #.

Learning the keyboard

There is an array of sheet music available on the internet for many of the pieces mentioned. Type the piece name into Google Images and add the words 'sheet music'. Another popular method of learning keyboard for young people is the keyboard tutorials on YouTube, for which there is a wide selection. Using this method, young people have more freedom to pick a piece that matches their ability and learn at their own pace.

Activity: Henri Mancini, *Pink Panther Theme* (RCA Victor, 1963)
Accompaniment: (# = black note to the right)

Part 1:	G# A A#	B	B A# A G#	G	G G# A A#
Part 2:	C# D D#	E	E D# D C#	C	C C# D D#

- 'Three Blind Mice' (trad., c. 1805)
- 'Animal Fair' (trad., 1898)
- 'Animal Crossing: New Leaf, Wild World' (Kazumi Totaka, Nintendo, 2001)

1.1.4 Improvisation
Activity 1: Animal passing

Stand in a circle. Choose an animal sound and pass it around the circle using your voice. When passing, you must use eye contact to show the next person it is their go. Next, add a second sound and let students choose which one to pass. Add a third or fourth. Pupils must try to remember who is which particular animal as they are now allowed to cross the circle to find their similar animal sound. Once they are successful they may stay next to that animal. In the end, all the animal sounds should be grouped together. To make it trickier, pupils must ask each other a question using the animal sounds, and the other pupil must respond in their animal voice. This helps pupils explore rhythm, pitch and timbre with their voice.

Activity 2: Journey of the 'Three Blind Mice'
On tuned percussion, or keyboards, teach the children the first 3 notes of 'Three Blind Mice' – B, A, G. Ask the students to compose music following a journey that the mice might take in finding some cheese. They must try to use only the 3 notes they have learnt but can use the elements of music to change their playing – tempo, pitch, dynamics, timbre, rhythm, harmony, texture, silence.

Activity 3: 'Baby Shark'
On tuned percussion or keyboards, teach children to play the 3 notes associated with the 'Baby Shark' song – D, E, G. Play around with the rhythms, or play a musical copycat game to help develop aural skills. Next get the pupils to choose another 3 notes and create their own rhythms. If it helps, the children can think of other baby animal names to use as inspiration for the rhythms they create, for example, baby cow, 'moo moo de moo de moo'.

1.1.5 Composition
Activity 1: Characterisation
Print out pictures of some of the animals used in *Carnival of the Animals*, for example lion, swan, elephant and kangaroo. Each table in the classroom must devise a piece of music to illustrate their chosen animal using whatever resources they have access to. The piece could tell the story of the average day of the animal, or simply illustrate the characteristics of the animal, for example slow, heavy, fast, hoppy. Pupils could also use onomatopoeia to create their compositions, for example words such as roar, screech, howl.

Activity 2: Stories
Choose a popular story about animals and get students to write a song or compose some illustrative music to show either the characterisation of the characters in the story or about the happenings in

the story. For example, the class could be split into groups and be given characters from *Winnie the Pooh* to compose a song for. Other stories including animals could include: *The Wind in the Willows; Alice in Wonderland; The Ugly Duckling.*

Activity 3: Poetry
Using poetry for musical inspiration has been happening for centuries. The following poems are suggestions for poems which could inspire young people to compose a creative piece using the musical elements to illustrate landscapes, stories or characters. Another idea is to create a music accompaniment for the poems to be spoken, or sung, over:

- 'The Owl and the Pussycat' (Edward Lear, 1871)
- 'The Tyger' (William Blake, 1794)
- 'At the Zoo' (A.A. Milne, 1924)
- 'The Spider and the Fly' (Mary Howitt, 1828)

Activity 4: Birdsong
Use the recording feature on a phone or iPad to capture some birdsong in the local neighbourhood. Compose music underneath the recordings, or to tell the story of the bird's journey. Listen to the opening of Vaughan Williams's *The Lark Ascending* (1914) for inspiration. Discuss how the composer uses the elements of music to illustrate the bird's journey, and then discuss how students could adapt their music compositions using similar methods.

Activity 5: Using sound effects
Most music software programmes have an array of sound effects and often animal sound effects. If you have access to iPads, then there are many sound effects apps, in particular animal apps. However, making animal sounds with our voices is always good fun and a popular favourite with young learners.

Activity 6: *Animal Farm*
In George Orwell's book *Animal Farm* (1945) the animals rebel against the farmer and take over the farm. The song 'Beasts of England' is sung by the animals to unite them in the act of rebellion. The song has many verses and is a good source of inspiration

for a class music composition. Introduce the lyrics to the students and give one or two verses to each group. They must compose a piece of music to accompany that verse and use their voices to add the lyrics, for example rap, with dance, using technology, a capella. After each group plays their version the class must decide on their favourite and try to learn the whole song in the favoured style.

1.2 WATER

1.2.1 Listening activities

Activity 1: 'Jaws Theme' from *Jaws* soundtrack (John Williams, MCA Records, 1975)

- What is the very first sound you hear before the shark theme enters? (*Low rumble*)
- How many notes are in the main shark theme? (*2 – E and F*)
- Why do they sound so suspenseful? (*Clashing notes played separately; semitone; dissonance; mimics the shark's heartbeat*)
- How does the music portray the shark getting closer? (*Getting faster; louder; the duration of the notes become shorter; more instruments join in so the texture builds; the notes are played with more accentuation; spikey*)

Activity 2: 'The Sailors' Hornpipe' from *Fantasia on British Sea Songs* (Sir Henry Woods, 1828)

- What instrument plays the tune first? (*Violin*)
- What woodwind instrument plays it next? (*Flute*)
- Describe the accompaniment: (*Plucking/pizzicato strings*)
- What happens to the tempo during the piece? (*Gets faster*)
- This piece is traditionally performed on the Last Night of the Proms. What instruments can the audience use to join in? (*Foghorns and party horns*)

Activity 3: *Vltava: Ma Vlast* – also known as *The Moldau or Die Moldau* (Bedřich Smetana, 1874)

This piece of music illustrates the flow and ebb of a river in Bohemia, which begins with two springs, one warm, one cold, which merge together. The single current flows through many landscapes, including meadows, woods, a farmer's wedding, mermaids in moonlight, past castles, ruins and palaces on rocks. The current then widens and swirls into rapids, flowing past Prague and disappearing into the Elbe river.

- At the beginning of the piece, the trickling water is represented by which woodwind instrument? (*Flute*)
- How are the strings being played in the introduction, with bows, or plucking? (*Plucking*)
- How does the woodwind create the feel of water flowing in a river? (*Ascending and descending scales with a pause at the top*)
- What family of instruments play the main tune (just after a minute in)? (*Strings*)
- How does the piece build up to represent the stream growing into a river? (*More instruments mean the texture grows; gets louder*)

Activity 4: 'Ocean's Bloom' – original soundtrack from the TV show *Blue Planet II* (Hans Zimmer and Radiohead, 2017)
- What is the first sound effect you hear? (*Water; waves lapping on the beach*)
- What instrument accompanies the voice when it begins? (*Cello*)
- How does this music represent the sound of the ocean?
  o *Overlapping beats/rhythms to give a sense of irregular patterns*
  o *Big sounds of the orchestra and quiet solo instruments*
  o *Lots of ethereal effects (resonance, panning) to create space and distance*
  o *Wave crashes*
  o *Building up and fading out to emulate the waves*

Activity 5: 'Water Walk' (John Cage, 1959)
Watch the video of John Cage's composition 'Water Walk' [https://youtu.be/gXOIkT1-QWY] performed live on a TV show. See how many unconventional instruments the pupils can list:

Bathtub, rubber duckie, 5 unplugged radios, water jug, iron pipe, goose call, and a grand piano.

Further listening
- 'La Mer' (Claude Debussy, L.109, 1905)
- 'Les jeux d'eaux a la Villa d'Este' (The Fountains of the Villa d'Este) (Franz Liszt, 1877)
- ' "Raindrop" Prelude' (Frederick Chopin, Op. 28, No. 15, 1838)

The BBC Ten Pieces website www.bbc.co.uk/teach/ten-pieces contains teaching resources for the following pieces of music linked to water:

- 'Night Ferry' (Anna Clyne, 2012)
- 'Sea Interludes: The Storm', from *Peter Grimes* (Benjamin Britten, 1945)

1.2.2 Singing
Vocal warm-ups
Use the following onomatopoeia words to create vocal warm-ups:

> drip, drop, pitter, patter, slurp, glug, sploosh, sprinkle, drizzle, spray

Tongue twister
'She sells seashells by the seashore, the shells she sells are seashells, I'm sure. So, if she sells seashells on the seashore, Then I'm sure she sells seashore shells.'

There are numerous songs with the theme of water. Here is a list of songs that work well with young students:

- 'Lowlands Away' (sea shanty) (Tyler Bryan, Ubisoft, 2013). Use the recordings from *Assassin's Creed IV* (game soundtrack – Sea shanties edition)
- 'Umbrella' (Rhianna, Def Jam, 2007)
- 'My Heart Will Go On', from *Titanic* (Celine Dion, 1997)
- 'Shiver Me Timbers', from *Muppet Treasure Island* (Hans Zimmer, 1996)
- 'Under the Sea', from *The Little Mermaid* (Alan Menken, 1989)
- 'Orinoco Flow' ('Sail Away') (Enya, WEA, 1988)

- 'The Rivers of Babylon' (Boney M, 1978; originally recorded by The Melodians, 1970)
- 'A Sailor Went to Sea, Sea, Sea' (Iona and Peter Opie, 1972)
- 'Bridge Over Troubled Water' (Simon and Garfunkel, Columbia, 1970)
- 'Raindrops Keep Fallin' on my Head' (Burt Bacharach, Scepter Records, 1969)
- '(Sittin' On) The Dock of the Bay' (Otis Redding, Volt, 1968)
- 'I Do Like to Be Beside the Seaside' (John A. Glover-Kind, 1907)
- '15 Men on a Dead Man's Chest', from *Treasure Island* (Robert Louis Stevenson, 1883)
- 'Blow the Man Down' (trad. c. 1860s)
- 'Drunken Sailor' (trad., c. early 19th century)

1.2.3 Playing
Activity 1: Theme from the *Pirates of the Caribbean*
The theme from Pirates of the Caribbean is quite tricky, but very well-known by most young people:

A, C, D, D, D, E, F, F, F, G, E, E, D, C, C, D

Activity 2: 'Drunken Sailor' (trad.)

Em 2 3 4	D 2 3 4	Em 2 3 4	Em D Em 4
What shall we do with the drunken sailor	What shall we do with the drunken sailor	What shall we do with the drunken sailor	Early in the morning
Em 2 3 4	D 2 3 4	Em 2 3 4	Em D Em 4
Hooray, and up she rises	Hooray, and up she rises	Hooray, and up she rises	Early in the morning

Other verses include:

Put him in the long boat till he's sober X 3
Early in the morning
Pull out the plug and wet him all over X3
Early in the morning

Shave his belly with a rusty razor X3
Early in the morning

Activity 3: 'We Are Sailing' (Rod Stewart, 1975; originally written by the Sutherland Brothers, 1972)
Chord sequence:

C, Am, F, C
D, Am, Dm, C/G

1.2.4 Improvisation
Activity 1: Water sound effects
Discuss what sound effects you might associate with water and create a brainstorm of onomatopoeia words on the board, for example splosh, drip, glug, pitter-patter. Think about in the bathroom, at the beach, or underwater. In groups, create a vocal sound piece to illustrate the building up of a storm, or a day at the beach.

Activity 2: Glass bottles
Collect some glass bottles and fill them with different amounts of water. Add a rainmaker (percussion instrument) and a thunder sheet (percussion). Create drip drop sounds using voices, or a tap. Create a graphic score or give each group a mood to portray – stormy, calm, building up, calming down. Let students take on the role of conductor as they select which groups should play, by pointing at the group, and waving their hands once to stop a group playing.

1.2.5 Composition
Activity 1: Writing sea shanties
Get students to imagine they are pirates on a boat at sea undergoing a treacherous journey. Tell them to write lyrics for a song to encourage the sailors not to give up hope on the journey. Brainstorm associated words on the board and get the pupils to form sentences, trying to create a story. Words might include: pirates, peg leg, rum, ship, Blackbeard, Jolly Roger, Kraken, walk the plank, yo ho ho,

mast, top-sail, mermaids, land ahoy. To add a simple accompaniment, choose 2 easy chords, for example, G major (G, B, D) and A minor (A, C, E).

Activity 2: Seascape graphic score

Discuss the physical nature and sounds of water at sea, from calm and peaceful, to turbulent and stormy. Listen to 'The Storm' from *Peter Grimes* by classical composer Benjamin Britten and analyse the mood of the sea by creating a timeline (extra resources on BBC Ten Pieces website, www.bbc.co.uk/teach/ten-pieces). Note down on the timeline when the music changes and ask students to describe how they think the sea is behaving. Create a graphic score of the sea, using visual symbols to depict the crashing waves, calmness, and sections where the sea builds up, or calms down. Once the graphic score is complete students can use the graphic score and their available instruments to create a piece that follows the same journey of the sea in the piece.

Activity 3: Using media

Using a film clip from the TV series *The Blue Planet II* and get students to compose a piece of music to accompany a given clip of video footage. Four examples of clips could be given to represent different moods:

- Shoals of fish shimmering before being eaten by a large predator
- Lurking sharks in the deep ocean
- Coral sea-life, tropical fish, seahorses, starfish, octopus, and crabs catching prey
- Penguins waddling and diving off cliffs in the Antarctic

1.2.6 Extra activities

Research topic: Whale song

Whales are known for their musicality, each one emitting their own song as a means of communication. Many scientists have studied the frequencies of whale song. Listen to examples of whale song on YouTube and research the reasons whales might communicate.

1.3 SPACE

1.3.1 Listening activities
Listening game: Theme music from TV shows

Play a range of TV theme tunes linked to shows about space and science-fiction. Pupils must list the themes they hear in the order they hear it. Pick music themes from the following list, depending on the age of your students:

- *Star Trek*
- *Dr Who*
- *The X-Files*
- *Thunderbirds*
- *Ben 10*
- *Futurama*
- *Stranger Things*

Activity 1: *The Planets* (Gustav Holst, 1914–16)

Gustav Holst composed *The Planets* between 1914 and 1916. The suite of music consists of 7 shorter pieces, each representing a different planet in astrology – Mars, Venus, Mercury, Jupiter, Saturn, Uranus, Neptune. *The Planets* has been embraced by music teachers as an excellent high-quality example of music characterisation. Play the following tracks and answer the associated questions:

'Mars, The Bringer of War'
- Describe the introduction – are the notes low/high? short/long? quiet/loud? (*Low, short, quiet*)
- How many beats are in a bar? (*5*)
- What role does the brass play in helping the piece develop? (*They create suspense*)
- Approximately 2 minutes in, the mood changes and the accompanying strings play straight crotchet beats. What typically non-orchestral brass instrument has the tune in this section? (*Euphonium*)

'Venus, The Bringer of Peace'
- What instruments play in the introduction? (*French horn, flutes*)
- How does Holst create a contrasting mood from Mars? (*High, long notes, quiet*)
- What role do the two harps play? (*Keep the beat*)

Activity 2: *Interstellar* (soundtrack) (Hans Zimmer, 2014)
Listen to some tracks from this acclaimed soundtrack and pick out the unusual orchestration – pipe organ, 4 pianos, synthesisers, computer. Zimmer wanted to capture the sound of the breath exhaling from the choir of 60 people to illustrate the notion of astronauts in space.

Main theme:

- What instrument starts the piece? (*Piano*)
- What family of instruments enters next? (*Strings*)
- How does the music build up to give the sense of a journey? (*More instruments, louder, larger texture, more parts*)

Activity 3: *Also Sprach Zarathustra, Op. 30* (Richard Strauss, 1896 – used in the soundtrack to Stanley Kubrick's film *2001: A Space Odyssey*)
- What instruments can you mostly hear? (*Timpani drums and brass*)
- How does the music build up? (*The dynamics get louder, the notes get higher, and more instruments enter to build the texture*)
- Is the tonality major (happy) or minor (sad)? (*Major*)
- What function does the lowest organ note serve? (*Drone*)

Activity 4: Music for *Star Wars* (John Williams, 1977 onwards). Compare and contrast character themes
- Listen to Darth Vader's theme in the Imperial March. How does John Williams capture the essence of evil? (*Loud brass fanfare, very ordered and structured, thick texture to show the voice of the army, minor key, attacking, accentuated notes*)
- Listen to Princess Leia's theme. How does John Williams characterise Princess Leia? (*Soft flute, major key, lots of expression in the*

musical phrases/sentences, slow tempo, soft dynamics, thin texture, harp, shimmering strings)
- How are the ewoks characterised in 'Parade of the Ewoks'? (*Jumpy, disjointed, punchy, short notes*)

Further listening
> *Guardians of the Galaxy*, soundtrack (Tyler Bates, 2014)
> *Gravity*, original motion picture soundtrack (Stephen Price, 2013)
> *Tron: Legacy*, soundtrack (Daft Punk, 2010)
> *Sun Rings* (Terry Riley, 2002). This is an album made with the Kronos Quartet. It features sounds of the planets recorded by the *Voyager* mission on its journey to Deep Space.

1.3.2 Singing
There are many songs associated with the idea of space:

- 'Super Massive Black Hole' (Muse, 2006)
- 'Men in Black' (Will Smith, 1997)
- 'Man on the Moon' (REM, 1992)
- 'Star Trekkin'' (The Firm, 1987)
- *The Dark Side of the Moon* album (Pink Floyd, 1973)
- 'Rocket Man' (Elton John, 1972)
- 'Space Oddity' (David Bowie, 1969),
- '(Is There) Life on Mars?' (David Bowie, 1971)
- 'Fly Me to the Moon' (Bart Howard, 1954; Frank Sinatra's version of this song was associated with the Apollo Missions in 1964)

1.3.3 Playing
There are many theme tunes to do with the topic of space. Here is a suggested list of themes that are enjoyable to learn with some guidance for which notes are in each theme:

Activity 1: Main Theme from the *Star Wars* soundtrack (John Williams, 1977)
> D, D, D, G-----, D (octave higher), C, B, A, G (octave higher), D

Activity 2: 'The Imperial March' from the *Star Wars* soundtrack (John Williams, 1977)

G, G, G, Eb, Bb, G, Eb, Bb, G

Activity 3: Main Theme from *E.T.* soundtrack (John Williams, 1982)

C, G, F, E, D, E, C, G – A, A, G, F#, E, F#, D, B

Activity 4: 'Clubbed to Death', from *The Matrix* soundtrack (Rob D, 2002)

Introduction:

Beats	1 2 3 4	1 2 3 4	1 2 3 4
Top part	Bb G C A	D Bb A C	Bb D G(8ve)
Lower part	G A	Bb C	D Eb
Beats	1 2 3 4	1 2 3 4	1 2 3 4
Top part	G F F Eb	D Bb G Bb A	
Lower part	B(natural) C	G C D	G

The BBC Ten Pieces website (www.bbc.co.uk/teach/ten-pieces) has some excellent notation materials for Holst's *Mars*.

1.3.4 Improvisation

Activity 1: Theme from *Close Encounters of the Third Kind* (John Williams, 1977)

Teach the pupils to play the 5 notes in the Theme from *Close Encounters of the Third Kind*: G, A, F, (octave lower) F, C. Play a musical question and answer game where you play a rhythm using one of the notes, and a student has to respond by playing a rhythm back. Add one more note each time until the caller is playing all 5 notes and the rhythmic pattern lasts more beats. The students can work in pairs to practice this musical communication game. For a harder level, use the second set of notes from the film: Bb, C, Ab, (octave lower) Ab, Eb.

Activity 2: *Also Sprach Zarathustra* (Richard Strauss, 1896)
Everybody play/sing the same note starting quietly, preferably the note C. After humming the next few notes, ask young people to see if they can work out the next notes on their instruments – G, C (octave higher). Using hand gestures (high, middle, low), direct students to change their notes. Can they make up a similar style piece that builds up too choosing 3–5 different notes?

Activity 3: Theme from *The X-Files* **(Mark Snow, 1993)**
Teach the first few notes of *The X-Files* theme tune – A, E, D, E, A (octave higher), E. Put the students in groups and ask each group to come up with rhythms based on the given notes. They can change the order, make the notes long or short, play high or low, combine notes or play in unison. Tell students to create a drone underneath.

1.3.5 Composition
Activity 1: Space poetry
Find a poem about space and use it for inspiration to compose a song. Decide on a rhythm and melody for the words to fit to. Next add a beat, whether clapping, or on drums. Next add chords, then instrumental fills in-between the verses. For a longer task, write the lyrics to your own space poem.

Activity 2: Journey of a space rocket
At the start of this activity the pupils may get inspiration from watching an Apollo mission launch, or the clip of Wallace and Gromit flying to the moon. Using whatever instruments and technology available get students to map the journey of a space rocket launch. The rocket can land on planets, disappear into black holes, meet aliens, have space battles or encounter a number of other space phenomenon. Students must then compose a piece of music to illustrate the journey. A good start would be to think of a heroic theme for the rocket and the launch. The theme could be adapted throughout the piece depending on what happens during the rocket's journey, for example it could be played faster, slower, higher, lower, louder, quieter, on different instruments or fragmented.

Activity 3: The Planets

After listening to Holst's *The Planets* give each group in the classroom a picture of a different planet or ask them to design their own planet. The pupils have to compose music to illustrate the different moods of each of the planets. As composers, decide on how the music should match the mood and character of the planet and then using the available instrumental resources compose music to fit with the character and mood of their planet.

1.3.6 Extra activities
Research activities

Research about any music played in space over the last few decades. Who has tried to get music played or recorded in space?

- In 1988 during the launch of the Soviet Soyuz TM-7, the musician David Gilmour (formally of Pink Floyd) claimed to make the first ever audio recording in space to be used in a future project.
- Will.I.Am wrote the song 'Reach for the Stars' for the landing of the Curiosity Rover on Mars in 2012. It was the first ever successful broadcast of music from another planet.
- Prior to this in 2003 Beagle 2 possibly broadcast a song by the UK band Blur; however there is no solid evidence as transmission back to Earth failed.
- Elon Musk launched a Tesla Roadster car into space during 2018 and used its sound system to loop the David Bowie songs, 'Space Oddity' and '(Is There) Life on Mars?'.

1.4 THE ENVIRONMENT AROUND US: SOUNDSCAPES AND SOUND MAPS

1.4.1 Listening
Activity 1

Tell students to close their eyes and listen to all the sounds around them. How many can they identify?

Typical sounds children will point out are as follows:

Bodily sounds: sniffing, breathing, coughing, sighing
Sounds in the classroom: tapping on tables, chairs shifting
Traffic from outside: planes, trains, cars, buses, beeping, screeches
The environment: birds

This is a good opportunity to teach about onomatopoeia – words that sound – for example: bang, sniff, hum, tick-tock, boom, oink.

Activity 2: '4' 33''' (John Cage, 1952)

In 1952, John Cage, a successful experimental composer composed a piece of music called '4' 33'''. The piece is in 3 sections and can be played by any instrument, or group of instruments. At the premiere performance a pianist simply sat at a piano and played nothing (videos are available on YouTube). The idea of the piece is to make the audience sit and engage with the sounds in the world around them. This is always an important exercise for young learners to do as it gives them an opportunity to think about what is happening in the world around them.

Activity 3: Sounds in the womb – www.hausdermusik.com/

Visit the website for the *Haus Der Musik* in Vienna which contains a recording of what it sounds like to be in a mother's womb. After listening to the sounds, ask pupils to describe what they can hear.

Activity 4: *Elements* (Ludovico Einaudi, 2015)

The Italian composer Ludovico Einaudi has composed many pieces in a meditative, purist style depicting elements of nature. His 2015 album *Elements*, and 2019 album *7 Days of Walking*, which portray the landscape and nature that surrounded Einaudi on a series of walks in the countryside. The track entitled 'Golden Butterflies' on Day 2 captures the fluttering wings of the butterflies. Compare this with the contrasting track 'Full Moon' on Day 5, which conveys night-time. Listen to some of the tracks with the students and ask them to give opinions and reasons as to whether they think the music matches the titles.

Further listening
- 'Earth' (Imogen Heap, 2009)
- *Earth* (Hans Zimmer, 2016) BBC Ten pieces

1.4.2 Singing
- 'Human' (Rag'n'Bone Man, 2017)
- 'Radioactive' (Imagine Dragons, 2012)
- 'Only Human' (Jason Mraz, 2008)
- 'Fake Plastic Trees' (Radiohead, 1995)
- 'Heal the World' (Michael Jackson, 1989)
- 'Earth Song' (Michael Jackson, 1995)
- 'What A Wonderful World' (Louis Armstrong, 1967)

1.4.3 Playing
Michael Jackson's 'Earth Song' (1995) works very well as a classroom ensemble piece.

Chords sequence
Verse:
Gm, C, Gm, C, Gm, C, D, D (x 2)
Chorus:
Eb, F, Bb, Bb, Cm, Cm, D, D

1.4.4 Improvisation
Activity 1: Meditation
Music for meditation and relaxation is a great soundscape to use for developing improvisation skills. The idea is to pick a major triad chord, for example, C-E-G and to introduce the notes very slowly, on instruments that can hold notes for a long time. If playing on tuned percussion, the notes will need to be softly struck again repeatedly. Below are some examples of chord sequences to improvise with. Students can move to the note changes in their own time, as slowly as possible.

Activity 2: Pentatonic improvisation – Minecraft
Create some atmospheric music based on a pentatonic scale (5 notes). Use the 5 notes to create an atmospheric piece similar

in style to the theme *C418* from the computer game *Minecraft*. If you have access to instruments with white notes, then improvise around the notes C-D-F-G-A, otherwise improvise using all 5 black keys.

1.4.5 Composition
Activity 1: School sound map

Send pupils around the school to record different sounds, either in words or using audio recorders. What does the environment sound like in the playground? The corridors? The lunch hall? Classrooms? The boiler room (with permission)? Next, they must draw a map of the school and draw the journey plus sounds they heard. Then they can devise and make a performance piece based on the sound map of the school. Pupils can swap their sound maps with each other and try to interpret each other's pieces.

Activity 2: The forest

Ask students to create a brainstorm of all the sounds they might expect to hear during a camping trip to a forest. Answers may include: frogs chirping, fires crackling, sausages sizzling, snoring, trees swaying, leaves rustling, bears, squirrels, crickets etc. Discuss how might the sounds of a rainforest be similar, or differ? If you have access to iPads use the *Samplebot app* for pupils to record sounds onto a soundboard. Once the sounds have been recorded, pupils can create their own forest composition.

1.5 JUNK PERCUSSION AND VEGETABLE ORCHESTRAS

1.5.1 Stomp – www.stomp.co.uk/

Originally formed in Brighton in 1991, Stomp now tour the world with their performances which use acrobatics, dance, circus skills, physical theatre, pantomime and music. Stomp are legendary at performing percussive music using everyday household items. Their philosophy is that you can make a sound with any everyday item – bins, brooms, pots, pans, zips, paper, cutlery.

Activity 1: Watching Stomp perform
Watch performances of Stomp and take note of what everyday items they are using in that particular performance.

Activity 2: Making instruments out of everyday items
This is a popular activity combining lots of skills and elements from science, and design technology. Research with the class how it is possible to use everyday items to make sounds. Suggestions for instruments to make are tin box guitars with rubber bands, glass water bottles filled with different levels of water, and shakers filled with dried beans or lentils.

Activity 3: Rhythms using school items
Find items around the school that can be used to create sounds, gather them together, and create a rhythmic piece. Choose a rhythm by creating sentences from the items collected, for example, 'pencil pots and rubbery rubbers' or 'crunchy paper in the air'. Ideas for playing include: building up the rhythmic layers; call and response; repetition; imitation.

Activity 4: The Vegetable Orchestra www.vegetableorchestra.org
The Vegetable Orchestra was formed in Vienna in 1998 and performs all over the world. They use food items to create sound and organise it together to make a piece of music.

The Viennese Vegetable Orchestra has recorded 4 albums: *Green Album, Onionoise, Automate* and *Gemise.* The website has fantastic short videos showing the individual instruments, live concerts and tours. These videos give a unique insight into the world of making music with vegetables. Issues such as non-transportability and lack of longevity mean the musicians have to re-carve their instruments for each performance. At the end of a concert the stage is pretty messy, and the audience end up having vegetable soup served to them after the performance.

Activity 5: Vegetable graphic scores
Using the idea of a graphic score, let students have colouring pens and paper to draw down the sounds they can hear. Play the first minute of any of the songs on the Viennese Vegetable Orchestra

albums and let students draw which vegetables they think they can hear, or any colours they can hear. The track 'Szemenye' is interesting as it is slightly reminiscent of a train.

Activity 6: Creating a vegetable orchestra

There are many videos on YouTube demonstrating how to carve out a vegetable orchestra. Common vegetables used to hollow out to make sounds are: carrot clarinet; pumpkin drum; pepper horn; leek violin.

Again, the idea here is to have fun exploring vegetables to find out if they can make a sound, and how expressive it is. The project does need consideration as there will be a need to use drills and sharp tools to carve out some of the holes; however, lots of vegetables need scooping out, which can be fun for students. Even the design element can be fun as children use their imaginations trying to work out how to create a sound out of each of the vegetables. Are there any other foods that would make great sounds? Muesli shakers? Jam jar glockenspiel?

Music is classed as 'organised sound'. Therefore, the idea of playing the music vegetable is to find a sound and build a piece out of repetition. Structure can be added by having clear sections of different vegetables.

CHAPTER 2
Music and storytelling

2.1 GRAPHIC SCORES

Graphic notation is a form of notation where you draw sounds using graphics and symbols. A graphic score is the piece of music created using graphics and symbols. Notating music and sound using pictures is more inclusive because everyone can interpret the pictures in their own way. Some pictures make more sense when representing sounds, others less so. For example, a line going up would typically represent sound going up in pitch rather than down. There may be a key, or short explanation, as to what the symbols/graphics in a graphic score represent musically. Sometimes there is no key and how to play the graphics is determined by the musician.

2.1.1 Listening activities
Graphic scores are visual, therefore listening activities must be accompanied by a visual in order to make more sense. There are many decent recordings with visuals that can be found on YouTube, including many examples of graphic score pieces made by students from all around the world, and classical pieces in graphic form.

Activity 1: *Stripsody* (Cathy Berberian, 1966)
• Listen and watch the performance on YouTube – 'Stripsody' (Cathy Berberian, 2010) https://youtu.be/0dNLAhL46xM
• Discuss opinions. Do the pupils think it is music or not? Why?

- Using print-outs of Cathy Beberian's graphic score, try to interpret some of the symbols.
- Pupils can have a go at performing their personal interpretations using Berberian's score.

Activity 2: Orchestral graphic scores – YouTube
Watch the graphic scores of a variety of orchestral works and discuss how graphics can demonstrate texture (number of parts) in music. Suggestions are:

- 'William Tell Overture' (Gioachino Rossini, 1829)
  YouTube: 'William Tell (Overture)' (Rossini), with animated graphic score by Stephen Malinowski (Smalin) [2 Jan. 2014]; https://youtu.be/1k8sGztMsKA
- *Symphony Number 5, Op. 67* (Ludwig Van Beethoven, 1804–8)
  YouTube: 'Beethoven, Symphony 5, 1st movement', with animated graphic score by Stephen Malinowski (Smalin) [15 July 2009]; https://youtu.be/rRgXUFnfKIY
- 'Winter' from *The Four Seasons* (Antonio Vivaldi, 1716–17)
  YouTube: 'Vivaldi, Winter, Four Seasons, Allegro)', with animated graphic score by Stephen Malinowski (Smalin) [7 June 2010]; https://youtu.be/Qqe0GdUpJHs

Activity 3: 'Thunderstorm', graphic score by Alex Chorley, aged 12
Watch Alex Chorley's graphic score on YouTube and take note of how he has illustrated some of the sounds in his composition. Ask pupils to design their own weather piece, considering how to represent the sounds using symbols or pictures.

YouTube: 'Thunderstorm', graphic score by Alex Chorley, aged 12, postedbyAlexChorley[2Sep.2013]https://youtu.be/bBawmitub64

2.1.2 Playing
Graphic scores are great fun to play, the best thing being that there is no such thing as playing it wrong. The aim is to give the best musical interpretation possible of the graphics and symbols. Because there is no incorrect way of playing a graphic score you have freedom and flexibility to give a personal interpretation. Find

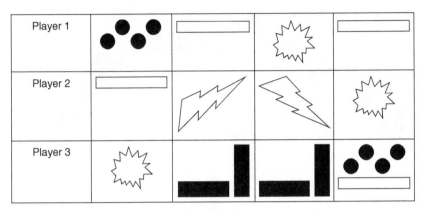

Figure 2.1 Music and storytelling

some basic graphic scores online or create your own in art. Decide on how the graphics might be interpreted using instruments.

2.1.3 Improvisation
Ask students how they could represent dynamics using pictures, or symbols. Once the concept has been learnt visually or kinetically, it can be transferred to the board or on paper and be represented by drawing a line or having a symbol either at different heights.

Activity 1: Vocal exploration
On the whiteboard, draw 3 lines (a stave). Draw shapes and patterns in-between these lines and then see if pupils can perform what you have drawn using their voices. Use different colour board pens for different parts. Develop the piece by adding phonic sounds.

Activity 2: Graphic score cards
Make a set of graphic score cards and then arrange them in different orders for the students to interpret musically.

2.1.4 Composition
Activity 1: Graphic score of a morning routine – based on Berberian's *Stripsody*
Ask pupils to give examples of sounds you might hear in the morning, for example brushing teeth, crunching cereal, alarm

31

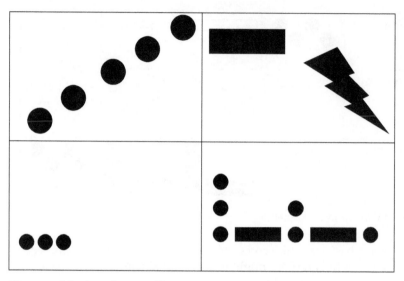

Figure 2.2 Music and storytelling

clock, birds singing. Be sure to make the sounds with your voice. Give students time to think of all of the sounds they personally hear in the morning, including programmes they watch on TV, other people's voices, sounds of pets. Tell the pupils to draw the sounds they hear, if possible in the order that they hear them, to create their own morning routine graphic score. The idea is that the students will practise their morning routine graphic scores and perform to the class, while reading from their own graphic score and graphic notation.

Activity 2: Treasure island map – graphic score and soundscape
Either give pupils a bird's eye view of a deserted treasure island or tell the pupils to design and draw their own island. Then let the students decide what sounds they can hear on the island and draw graphics to represent the sounds. This could include:

- Wildlife on the island such as parrots and monkeys
- The sounds of the environment, waves, wind, storms

- The sounds on the ship – Cannons firing, pirates jeering.
- Treasure chest and coconut palms
- Kraken and sharks

They can then chart their journey from the pirate ship to the treasure, and then back again. Students can use instruments, their voices and body percussion to create a piece of music depicting the journey. They must portray the mood and atmosphere of the journey and any sounds they might hear. They can incorporate a short sea shanty too if they choose.

For an extension task, get the pupils to draw grid lines on the picture of the island and use the map coordinates to plot an order for the sounds. They can then give each other coordinates to compose pieces of music.

Activity 3: Haunted house graphic score
Provide students with a template of an old spooky looking house. Pupils use instruments and their voices to create a story of events that evolve in the haunted house. For example, the story could show the adventures of a person walking through the haunted house; of a lonely ghost trying to make friends; or a well-known character such as Count Dracula, or Frankenstein.

Activity 4: Emoji graphic score
Print out lots of pictures of emojis. Students must build a story and create a graphic score, using all of the different emojis. Next work out how to play the graphic score using instruments or voices.

Activity 5: Superhero graphic score
Get some inspiration from superhero comics. Cut out and create a graphic score using pictures from the comics. Use comic writing to put in action words such as, *kapow, whack, bang* and *zap*. See if the graphic score can tell one of the stories of the superhero.

2.2 SONGWRITING

Songwriting is a creative tool for self-expression. Songs are written about a variety of topics, from friendship and love, to everyday events. Commonly songs are written about emotions (for example happiness or sadness), and telling stories, whether about day to day happenings, or mythical events.

2.2.1 Listening
Activity: Structure in popular songs

Understanding musical structures is an important place to start when songwriting. The best way to learn about song structure is to listen to pop songs, which have very basic and clearly defined structure.

The different sections are: Introduction (intro), pre-chorus, chorus (or refrain), verse (V), bridge (middle 8) and outro.

Listen to the following 3 pop songs and break down the structure of each song:

- 'Happier' (Marshmello ft. Bastille, 2018) – Intro, Chorus, V1, Chorus, V2, Middle 8, Chorus
- 'Believer' (Imagine Dragons, 2017) – Intro, V1, Chorus, V2, Chorus, V3, Chorus
- 'Uptown Funk' (Mark Ronson, 2014) – Intro, V1, Chorus, V2, Middle 8, V3 Chorus, outro
- 'Reach for the Stars' (S Club 7, 2000) – Intro, V1 Chorus, V2, Chorus, Middle 8, Chorus

Repeat this exercise with some of the pupils' favourite songs.

2.2.2 Singing

Once you have written the lyrics of a song it is a good idea to either sing the song yourself or teach other people how to sing your song. Performances help people to develop good rehearsal techniques as they provide deadlines for people to learn music by. Performances can be to a friend, to another teacher, to parents, to another class, and take place in school, or if transport is available, at a different location.

2.2.3 Playing
Activity 1: Composing accompaniments using technology
Writing an accompaniment for the song lyrics to be sung over is not as tricky as it might seem, especially with access to apps and mobile technologies. There are a range of apps that enable the beginner songwriter to create beats, bass riffs and chords, either by providing pre-composed samples or by having a very simple tool to aid composition. Apple's *GarageBand* app is an excellent place to start for the budding songwriter as it gives an option of samples, or 'smart' instruments. The 'smart' instruments option is superb as the chords for each instrument offered are easily accessible to play in a variety of styles.

If you have access to an iPad, the *Chord Generator* app is helpful in generating chord sequences for budding songwriters. The *Suggester* app by Mathieu Routhier gives examples of higher-level chord progressions.

Activity 2: Playing chord sequences
A chord sequence is a series of chords played in succession one after the other. Some chord sequences sound better than others, so here are a few suggestions to help get started:

- C, F, G
- Em, C, G, D
- G, Em, C, G
- C, Am, F, G

Songwriter lyrics Pro is another useful app and focuses on the lyric writing aspect of songwriting.

2.2.4 Improvisation
Activity 1: MC-ing

MC-ing is a great creative method of improvising as it requires the ability to explore words, and create lyrics, on the spot. Hand out some easy to rhyme words and get pupils to try and make as many sentences as possible using the words. Then in pairs, get one person to keep a beat (tapping a drum, beat-boxing, clicking fingers) while the second person tries to give the sentences more rhythm by trying to say the sentences more in time with the beat.

Activity 2: Rap battles

Rap battles are a fun exercise for coming up with words on the spot. Pick a topic, such as chocolate bars, football, or school, and get two students to rap on the spot over a beat in competition with each other. The rest of the class can keep a beat going for the rappers to rap over. This can also be done in small groups.

2.2.5 Composition
Activity 1: Methods for songwriting

There are 2 main methods for effective songwriting composition in the classroom. Firstly, write the lyrics before you choose or compose the music. Secondly, compose the music before writing the lyrics. It is personal preference as to which you may choose and sometimes a particular method suits a specific purpose. For example, you could use a karaoke song as a musical background and may need to write lyrics that fit with the precomposed tune and rhythms.

Activity 2: Song themes

Here is a list of typical song ideas for schools:

Environment – weather, oceans

Countries – national anthems, folk songs

School issues – homework, bullying, internet safety, canteen food, subjects, teachers

Emotions – love, happiness, fun, depression, the blues, fear, revenge, power

People – celebrities, families, friends, relationships, teachers, siblings

There are many soap dramas on TV to pick a story from or alternatively use a film, piece of celebrity gossip, or sports event for inspiration.

Once a theme or story has been selected to write a song, use a thesaurus to brainstorm lots of words associated with that topic.

Activity 3: Rhyming song lyrics
Select words from the brainstorm and try to find rhyming words. Then put these into sentences. The aim is to then put these sentences over a beat, either by clicking, clapping, or using a beat on technology. Once you are happy with the rhythm, add melody notes to complete the phrase.

2.3 MUSICALS

The most popular theatres to watch musicals are in the West End in London, and Broadway in New York, USA. Many people enjoy performing musicals and so there are numerous community theatre groups. It is usual for schools to perform musicals. In the past people had to visit a theatre, however, nowadays, because of technological advancements, young people can access musicals in a variety of ways, such as at the cinema, online or on TV. Musicals are celebrated globally, and Bollywood produces more big-budget musicals every year with huge commercial success.

This topic can be really bolstered by taking the students on a trip to see a musical at a theatre. There they can learn about theatres and experience what it is like to be a member of an audience. This is an important cultural experience for students to learn about community and the arts, particularly in musical theatre, technical theatre and performance.

Activity 1: Types of musicals – research
Musicals are made using a variety of different mediums for a range of different audiences. The table below has separated musical types into: theatre; film; animation/cartoon; and Bollywood. Give

a blank table to pupils and get them to fill in as many answers for each of the columns.

Theatre	Film	Animation/ cartoon	Bollywood
Les Misérables	La La Land	Frozen 1 & 2	Dangal
The Lion King	The Greatest	Happy Feet	Bajrangi Bhaijaan
Phantom of	Showman	Trolls	Secret Superstar
the Opera	West Side Story	Sing	PK
Wicked	Sister Act	Aladdin	Sultan
Miss Saigon	Grease		Sanju
Evita	High School		
My Fair Lady	Musical		
Kiss Me Kate	Mary Poppins		
Chess	Mamma Mia		
Guys and Dolls	School of Rock		
Hamilton			

Activity 2: Stories in musicals

The key factor in a musical is the story, whether it be a theme of romance, comedy or thriller. Songs can be solos, duets, or sung by choruses, with spoken dialogue in-between each song. Similarly to opera, songs can have two main purposes, to convey the character's emotions, or to add to the plot and push it forward.

Print out a sheet with many images from musicals and get pupils to cut them out. The pupils must choose a musical to research the story and find at least 2/3 famous songs from the musical.

Activity 3

Write a synopsis for a brand new 'hypothetical' musical. Use songs from existing musicals to portray the storyline in your new musical. See how many musicals you can reference through the song choices.

2.3.1 Listening activities
Activity 1: 'Hakuna Matata' from *The Lion King* (Elton John, 1995)
- What does the phrase 'Hakuna matata' mean? (*No worries*)
- What tuned percussion instrument can you hear in the introduction? (*Xylophone*)
- Describe the vocal style: singing, speaking or both (*Both*)
- What keyboard instrument features in the accompaniment? (*Accordion*)

Activity 2: 'A Million Dreams' from *The Greatest Showman* (Benj Pasek and Justin Paul, Atlantic, 2017).
- What instrument starts the piece? (*Piano*)
- How is the accompaniment being played, held chords or broken chords? (*Broken chords*)
- What family of instruments comes in next? (*Strings*)
- What instrument plays the accompaniment at the beginning of verse 2? (*Guitar*)

Activity 3: 'My Favourite Things' from *The Sound of Music* (Julie Andrews, 1965) – compare and contrast
Listen to the original version and then listen to one or more of the other versions of the song:

- '7 Rings' (Ariana Grande, 2019) – clean version
- 'My Favourite Things' (Big Brovas, 2002) – rap, accordion, hip-hop
- 'My Favourite Things', title track from *My Favourite Things* (John Coltrane, 1961) – jazz, saxophone, piano, double bass, swung rhythms, no singing

Activity 4: *West Side Story* (Leonard Bernstein, 1961)
The songs in *West Side Story* encompass a range of musical styles and portray a range of moods. Listen to the first minute of some of the following songs and ask students to describe the mood/character of the songs:

- 'Tonight', 'One Hand, One Heart', 'Maria' – love, long notes, lyrical, stepwise
- 'I Feel Pretty', 'Gee Officer Krupke' – happy, skippy, short and long, lots of words

- 'A Boy Like That' – anger, very accented, sharp, spikey, angular
- 'One Hand, One Heart' – sad, long, lyrical, minor
- 'Dance at the Gym' – jazz, funky, Latin-American rhythms, off-beats

Orchestration: Bernstein has added some instruments which are not typical for a traditional orchestra, can you hear what they are? (bass clarinet, drum kit, saxophone)

2.3.2 Singing

There are many resources to use for learning songs from musicals, from karaoke backing tracks to orchestral scores. You may want to perform just one or two numbers or put on a whole school show. Below is a list of suggested musicals which work well in school for ages 7–14:

- *High School Musical* (2006) Disney
- *School of Rock* (2003) Paramount Pictures
- *The Lion King* (1994) Disney (be prepared to learn songs in a different language)
- *Grease* (1978) Paramount Pictures
- *Wizard of Oz* (1939) Metro-Goldwyn-Mayer

Popular songs from musicals for all ages:

- 'Shallow', from *A Star is Born* (Lady Gaga and Bradley Cooper, 2018)
- 'A Million Dreams', 'Rewrite the Stars', 'This is Me', from *The Greatest Showman* (Pasek and Paul, 2017)
- 'City of Stars', from *La La Land* (music by Justin Hurwitz, lyrics by Pasek and Paul (2016)
- 'How Far I'll Go', from *Moana* (Auli'i Cravalho, 2016)
- 'Cup Song', from *Pitch Perfect Soundtrack* (Anna Kendrick, 2012)
- 'Let It Go', 'Vuelie', 'Do You Want to Build a Snowman?', from *Frozen* (Lopez, 2013)
- 'Angel of Music', 'All I Ask of You', from *The Phantom of the Opera* (Andrew Lloyd Webber, 1986)

- 'I Dreamed a Dream', 'Castle on a Cloud', from *Les Misérables* (Claude-Michel Schoenberg, 1980)
- 'It's a Hard Knock Life', 'Tomorrow', from *Annie* (Charles Strouse, 1976)
- 'Food Glorious Food', 'Consider Yourself', 'Who Will Buy', You've Got to Pick a Pocket or Two from *Oliver!* (Lionel Bart, 1960)
- 'A Spoonful of Sugar', 'Chim Chim Cheree', 'Super-cali-fragil-istic', from *Mary Poppins* (Richard and Robert Sherman, Buena Vista, 1964)
- 'Do-Re-Mi', 'Edelweiss', 'My Favourite Things', from *The Sound of Music* (Richard Rodgers and Oscar Hammerstein II, RCA Victor, 1965)

2.3.3 Playing

Activity: 'Rock Got No Reason', from *School of Rock* (2003)

School of Rock is particularly great if your students play any instruments in a rock band or can access keyboards. Listen to the song and try to play along with the following chord sequence. Practise slowly at first, then speed up. Also rehearsing over a YouTube clip of the song can help with practising.

Verse 1

D, C, B, C x 3
D, C, G

Chorus

D, E, G, D x3
D, C, G

Activity 2: 'When I'm Gone (Cup Song)', from *Pitch Perfect* (Anna Kendrick, 2012)

'Cup Song' by Anna Kendrick is a lovely song for children to learn. Start off by learning the vocal part, then learn the cup rhythm part separately. Allow children time to practise very slowly and then speed up. In pairs or groups, one part can play the cup rhythm, the other can sing. Some children may even end up being able to do both at the same time once they have mastered the coordination skills.

2.3.4 Improvisation

Choose several phrases from well-known musicals and use them to create rhythmic patterns. For example:

'I'd like to pick a pocket or two' (*Oliver*)
'Hakuna Matata is a wonderful phrase' (*The Lion King*)
'Let it go, let it go, don't hold it back anymore' (*Frozen*)

Play these rhythms (even use picture cards held up) and layer an improvisation. Stick picture cards on the board to suggest an order for the rhythms to be played. Let the students add new phrases and create new rhythms to add.

2.3.5 Composing
Activity 1
Choose your favourite song from a musical and print out the lyrics. Try to compose a new melody and accompaniment for the lyrics.

Activity 2
Write your own musical. This is a longer project and would require lots of time dedicated to it. It is possible to do it as a class, with pupils making decisions about the story and script. Small groups could have the responsibility of writing the script for different scenes. Young people could choose suitable songs to accompany their scenes, or compose original songs, depending on ability.

Activity 3
Some musicals are based around the life stories of musicians or bands such as Abba and Queen.

Choose your favourite musician/singer/band and create a musical based on their life story.

2.3.6 Extra activities
Research activity
Pick one of the most well-known musical writers and research which musicals they wrote:

- Rodgers and Hammerstein
- Andrew Lloyd Webber
- Gilbert and Sullivan
- Cole Porter
- Stephen Sondheim
- Kander and Ebb

2.4 FOLK MUSIC

Every country in the world has its own folk music which celebrates the nationalism of the people and landscapes of the country through music. Often traditional folk songs are anonymous, associated with the community, and passed orally through generations, often expressing nationality through the music. Typical folk instruments are: acoustic guitar, flute, penny whistle, folk fiddle/violin, harp, bodhran (Irish drum), bagpipes, accordion, mandolin and banjo. Types of folk songs include a range of music for the people: ballads telling local stories with themes of love, adventure and mystery; national anthems; football chants; children's songs and nursery rhymes.

2.4.1 Listening activities
Activity 1: Folk music of the British Isles
Put a picture to represent the four countries in Great Britain on the four walls. Play folk music from each of these countries and students have to move to which wall they think the music belongs to.

England	Morris dancing music; 'Country Gardens'; 'Brigg Fair'
Scotland	Highland music and lowland music; bagpipes; 'My Bonnie Lies Over the Ocean'; 'I will Walk 100 Miles' (The Proclaimers)
Wales	'Men of Harlech'; Welsh harp songs
Ireland	'Danny Boy'; The Dubliners; 'The Irish Washerwoman'; *Riverdance*; mostly music played in pubs with drinking and socialising – the 'craic'

Activity 2: Folk instrument listening game

Play excerpts of music played by the following traditional folk instruments and students have to guess the name of the instrument they are listening to: bagpipes, banjo, accordion, Irish fiddle, Celtic harp, harmonica, penny whistle, concertina, bodhran, mandolin.

Activity 3: 'Fantasia on Greensleeves' (Ralph Vaughan Williams, 1934)

- Which 2 instruments play at the start? (*Harp and flute*)
- Which family of instruments play the theme? (*Strings*)
- When the mood changes, which family of instruments then play the theme? (*Lower strings*)
- When the flutes play the theme, how is the accompaniment played by the strings, plucking (pizzicato) or with the bow (arco)? (*Plucking/pizzicato*)
- What is the time signature? How many beats are in each bar? (*6/8–6 quaver beats in a bar*)

Activity 4: 'The Times They Are a-Changin'' (Bob Dylan, 1964)

Listen to three versions of this song by different artists, comparing the similarities and spotting the differences:

Bob Dylan (1964)	The Seekers (1965)	Phil Collins (1996)
Acoustic guitar Strumming chords Folk-style singing Mouth organ/ harmonica	Lots of voices male/ female Singing in harmony Double bass	Piano accompaniment Pop-style singing Drum-kit Synthesiser Electric guitar Bass guitar

2.4.2 Singing

There are lots of folk songs to choose from. Here is a selection covering many decades and styles:

- 'I Will Wait' (Mumford and Sons, 2012)
- 'Rambling Man' (Laura Marling, 2010)
- 'Black Horse and the Cherry Tree' (KT Tunstall, 2005)

- 'All Around My Hat' (Steeleye Span, 1975, originally 19th century, trad.)
- 'Streets of London' (Ralph McTell, 1969)
- 'Turn, Turn, Turn' (Pete Seeger, 1959)
- 'If I Had a Hammer' (Pete Seeger, 1950)
- 'She'll Be Comin' Round the Mountain' (Carl Sandburg, 1927)
- 'Danny Boy' (Frank Weatherly, 1910)
- 'Scarborough Fair' (trad. English ballad, c. 19th century)
- 'Like a Rolling Stone', 'Blowin' in the Wind', 'Masters of War' (Bob Dylan)
- 'My Bonnie Lies Over the Ocean' (trad. Scottish ballad, 19th century)

2.4.3 Playing
Activity 1: 'My Bonnie Lies Over the Ocean' (trad. 19th century)
Notes for the melody in the verse:

G, E, D, C, D, C, A, G, E
G, E, D, C, C, B, C, D
G, E, D, C, D, C, A, G, E
G, A, D, C, B, A, B, C

Activity 1: 'Country Gardens' (Percy Grainger, 1918)

D	D C# B	B	A	A G F# F# G	A	D	E	G	F#	E	D
D	G		A	D	D	Em			A		D

2.4.4 Improvisation
Activity 1: Two chords
Folk music often uses a simplistic chord sequence as it is meant to be easy to play and for people to improvise over. Learning just two chords (C/Dm, Dm/Em, F/G, G/Amin work well), create an accompaniment by adding rhythm and structure. Repeat the chord sequence and get other people to learn it too.

Activity 2: Modes and drones
Many traditional folk songs were composed in times when modes were more popular for songwriting. Use the notes of the Dorian

mode – D, E, F, G, A, B, C – to compose a folk tune. Build an accompaniment using the drone note of – D, adding perhaps the 4th or 5th notes too – G, or A. For an extension write a set of folk lyrics about an urban legend.

2.4.5 Composition
Activity 1: Write a folk ballad
Folk ballads are written about dramatic events or stories, such as stories from war or battles, mythical legends, lovers and betrayal, sailors at sea, seasons, magical characters. Choose a folk poem or story to turn into a folk ballad by creating adding rhythms and melodies. Use the well-known tune of a recognisable song to fit the new lyrics into, for example, 'The Animals went in Two by Two', or 'Greensleeves'.

Activity 2: Protest music – write a protest song
Many young people today are aware that songs can convey messages of protest about political, global and environmental issues. Grime music and powerful raps written by modern-day artists such as Stormzy have reaffirmed youth voice and reignited the powerful medium song can be for speaking up for, or against, topical issues. Traditionally folk music was used to convey messages of protest and the style of songwriting lent itself naturally to conveying both the artist's and general public opinion of dissatisfaction.

Listen to famous protest songs by artists such as Bob Dylan, Pete Seeger and Joan Baez. Create a brainstorm of issues that you are unhappy about in the world and would like to change. They could be local issues, such as issues in the school community, or local community, or global issues such as global warming or poverty. In pairs/groups decide on an issue that you would like to protest about. Write verses to give examples of things that have happened (telling the story) and the chorus to convey how you feel (mood and emotion) about the issue.

2.4.6 Dancing
Activity: Dancing
Learn a traditional folk dance – ceilidh, Morris dance, maypole dance, Riverdance

2.4.7 Research
Activity: Research music of the British Isles
Research folk music in these countries and explain what is meant by the given terms:

Ireland – the 'craic', 'sessions'
Wales – The National Eisteddfod Society, Urdd Eisteddfod
Scotland – Ceilidh dances, Scottish country dances
England – Morris dancing

Make a travel show by exploring the folk music of the British Isles.

2.5 PROGRAMME MUSIC – SYMPHONIC POEMS

Many composers in the late 19th century composed pieces of instrumental music which represented stories from literature, art, poetry, folk tales, myths and legends. This genre of classical music is called 'programme music' and refers to compositions called 'tone poems' or 'symphonic poems'. Programme music uses musical techniques to convey moods and characterisations to depict a non-musical stimulus, making this body of work a valuable resource when teaching young people about mood and tension in music. It really precedes film music of today.

2.5.1 Listening activities
Activity 1: 'Danse Macabre, Op. 40' (Camille Saint-Saëns, 1874)
'Danse Macabre' is a piece for violin and orchestra based on a poem by Henri Cazalis. It tells the tale of the dead rising from their graves at night, luring the living to their doom by conjuring up a deathly dance. As the clock strikes midnight Death arises and plays the violin to awaken the skeletons. They dance to a waltz which builds and builds, finally returning back to their graves once the cock crows to signify dawn.

- How many chimes does the harp play? What time does it represent? (*12*)
- How many beats are in the bar for the dance? (*3 beats in a bar*)

- What instrument illustrates the sound of the skeleton bones? (*Xylophone*)
- (Higher level) What interval is the violinist using to tune up? (*Augmented 4th/diminished 5th – tritone*)
- What instrument represents the cock-crowing? (*Oboe*)

Activity 2: *Scheherazade, Op. 35* (Nikolai Rimsky-Korsakov, 1888)
This tone poem is based on stories from *The Arabian Nights* (also known as *One Thousand and One Nights)*

- Is the opening theme descending or ascending? (descending)
- After the initial theme what family of instruments play the block chords? (woodwind)
- What instrument represents the princess Scheherazade? (violin)
- What instrument accompanies the solo instrument? (harp)

Activity 3: *Pictures at an Exhibition* (Modest Mussorgsky, 1874)
Listen to the orchestral arrangement by Maurice Ravel (1922) of *Pictures at an Exhibition*, a suite of 10 pieces inspired by art created by Mussorgsky's friend Viktor Hartmann who passed away suddenly. The titles of the pieces are:

The 'Promenade' starts the piece and also plays between some of the shorter pieces.

1. 'The Gnome'
2. 'The Old Castle'
3. 'Children's Quarrel after Games (Tuileries)'
4. 'Cattle'
5. 'Ballet of Unhatched Chicks'
6. ' "Samuel Goldenberg" and "Schmuÿle" '
7. 'Limoges. The Market (The Great News)'
8. 'Catacombs (Roman Tomb) – With the Dead in a Dead Language'
9. 'The Hut on Hen's Legs (Baba Yaga)'
10. 'The Great Gate of Kiev'

Listen to the 'Promenade':

o What orchestral family of instruments start the piece? (*Brass*)
o Do they play all together in harmony or play lots of different parts? (*All together*)
o Which family of instruments plays next? (*Strings*)
o Do the strings and brass play together at any point in the piece? (*Yes, the final time the theme is played*)

Activity 3: *Symphonie Fantastique, Op.14* (Hector Berlioz, 1830)
Listen to each of the five movements from *Symphonie Fantastique* and discuss how Berlioz has created the related moods:

   I. 'Rêveries – Passions' (Reveries – Passions) – C minor/ C major
   II. 'Un bal' (A Ball) – A major
   III. 'Scène aux champs' (Scene in the Fields) – F major
   IV. 'Marche au supplice' (March to the Scaffold) – G minor
   V. 'Songe d'une nuit du sabbat' (Dream of a Night of the Sabbath)

Has he been successful in creating different moods through the music? How has Berlioz achieved this? Discuss opinions and reasons why.

For an extension composition task, split the class into 5 groups and allocate each group a movement from Berlioz's symphony. Each group must compose a piece of music to represent the titled theme of the given movement.

2.5.2 Playing
Use the BBC Ten Pieces website to find notation resources for the following pieces of programme music. Watch the video clips which have been made to tell the stories dramatically to convey the meaning of the music to young people:

• *Ride of the Valkyries* (Richard Wagner, 1856)
• *Night on the Bare Mountain* (Modest Mussorgsky, 1867)
• *The Firebird* (Igor Stravinsky, 1910)
• *Carmen* (Georges Bizet, 1875)

2.5.3 Composition
Activity 1: Illustrating a fairy-tale using music

Choose a fairy-tale and give a synopsis of the story to the class. Split the class into smaller groups. Give each group a character to represent and allow time for each group to create a musical idea to represent that character. Read the fairy-tale out loud and encourage each group to play their musical ideas when their character is mentioned. On reading through the second time, see if the class can play the story without words. For example:

- *Hansel and Gretel* would need a musical idea for the following characters: Hansel, Gretel, the witch, wicked stepmother, father.
- *Snow White* would need music to portray Snow White, the wicked stepmother, 7 dwarves, Prince Charming
- *Little Red Riding Hood* – Little Red Riding Hood, the Wolf, Grandma, Father

Some of the characters would need to show different emotions so encourage students to find a way of playing their musical idea in different ways (using the elements of music) to present each emotion.

Activity 2: Illustrating a poem using music

Many poems provide a set of lyrics for somebody to compose music to. Learning how to add a melody and make a simple accompaniment is a good skill. Here is a selection of poems from a range of time periods in different styles:

> 'Chocolate Cake' (Michael Rosen, 2017)
> 'Dog on the Playground' (Allan Ahlberg, 2008)
> 'The Owl and the Pussycat' (Edward Lear, 1871)
> 'Jabberwocky' (Lewis Carroll, 1871)
> 'I Wandered Lonely as a Cloud' (William Wordsworth, 1802)

Activity 3: Illustrating a legend using music

Some composers have turned to the inspiration of legends to compose music.

Many composers, including Liszt and Berlioz, composed orchestral works based on the legend of Faust by Goethe. Here is a list of legends to use for inspiration for a composition project: Atlantis; Robin Hood; King Arthur; El Dorado; The Fountain of Youth; Lady Godiva; David and Goliath.

Activity 4: Illustrate a painting using music
Some paintings lend themselves to being great inspiration for composers, for example Mussorgsky's *Pictures at an Exhibition*. Get pupils to research their favourite artists and paintings. Encourage them to describe what they see and interpret the story behind the painting using words. Work out which characteristics, or story, can be told through music and using the resources at hand try to convey the mood, story and character of the painting. After pupils perform their piece, it does not necessarily need any explanation, although sometimes students are proud to explain the thought process behind their music compositions.

Activity 5: *The Four Seasons* (Antonio Vivaldi, 1716–17)
Split the class into four groups and give each group a season. Each group must brainstorm words to do with the imagery and events linked to the season and write a set of lyrics for a song. They can also compose an accompaniment for the song lyrics to be read or sung over. Try adding sound effects for the different seasons using voices, percussion, or technology.

CHAPTER 3
Music and history

3.1 MEDIEVAL MUSIC

Medieval music began in the 5th century with the fall of the Roman Empire and lasted until the 15th century. During this period of 1000 years, music was classed as either *secular* or *sacred* music, meaning non-religious or religious music.

Secular songs were sung while working in the fields, at parties and feasts, and in the home. News, stories, political propaganda and gossip were spread from village to village by travelling minstrels who were skilled songwriters and lute players. Troubadours were royal performers who would play music, read poetry and compose songs in the royal court. Alongside the troubadours were the jongleurs, who would sing songs written by the troubadours, and perform by juggling, conjuring, dancing, singing, storytelling and doing acrobatics.

Sacred music happened in churches and consisted of plainsong and plainchant sung in Latin text by monks.

Although there are no authentic recordings of Medieval music, only modern-day interpretations, some surviving manuscripts have helped musicologists to learn about Medieval music. They have found out that Medieval music has the following characteristics:

- One line of melody/tune (monophonic)
- Modal tonality (in modes, not keys)
- No accompaniment (so no bassline or chords)
- It typically had 3/6 beats in a bar

- Much of the music was expected to be improvised (made up on the spot)

3.1.1 Listening
Activity 1: Gregorian chant

Gregorian chants, named after Pope St Gregory the Great, were most commonly sung without accompaniment – a capella. These chants were also known as plainsong or plainchant and were sung in Latin, mainly due to the Catholic Church's prominence in this period of history. Monks would gather around one manuscript to sing and let their voices resonate out in the vast spaces of the church. Listen to the Gregorian chant – 'Deum Verum' by the composer Etienne De Liege https://youtu.be/kK5AohCMX0U [4 Feb. 2010]:

- Are the voices male or female? (*Male*)
- Is the opening plainchant monophonic (one vocal line) or polyphonic (2 or 3 vocal lines interweaving)? (*Monophonic*)
- Describe the accompaniment. (*There is no accompaniment*)
- When the second line of singing enters do the voices sing the same notes in unison, or do they sing in harmony? (*In harmony*)

Activity 2: Medieval English folk song

The 'Agincourt Carol' is an English folk song written in the 15th century about the battle of Agincourt. Listen to the version recorded by the group Poxy Boggards:

YouTube: 'Agincourt Carol' Poxy Boggards [6 Dec. 2017] posted by God, King, and Country; https://youtu.be/k9WZO4W1be4:

- Are the singers male, or female? (*Male*)
- Are the rhythms straight, or swung? (*Swung*)
- Do the singers sing in unison, or polyphony? (*Unison*)
- What happens to the accompaniment when the singers sing in a different language 'Deo gratias'? (*There is no accompaniment*)
- How many beats are in a bar? (*6 quaver beats, 6/8*)

The song is in a minor sounding mode, but the last chord of the song is in a major key. This is called a '*tierce de picardie*' and has the function of leaving the listeners with a happy feeling, especially after songs in church where there is a lot of resonance.

Traditional western classical notation – crotchets and quavers – derive from the Medieval notation used by the monks in these times. Real gold leaf would be used to adorn the manuscripts, which were made from thinly stretched animal skins.

Towards the end of the Medieval period the single line melody grew and a second, or third melodic line was added as another musical layer. This musical texture is called polyphony (many parts).

Activity 3: 'Veni Sancte Spiritus' (John Dunstable, 1390–1453) [17 June 2017];
https://youtu.be/9dYAEpf-A-A

- Are the voices male or female? (*Male, including boys' voices*)
- Describe the accompaniment. (*There is no accompaniment*)
- Are the vocal parts sung in unison, homophony (parts moving together), or polyphony (parts interweaving)? (*Polyphony*)
- Further listening: Compare this to the version by the contemporary composer *Arvo Pärt*.

Activity 4: Medieval instruments
Listen to a range of Medieval instruments and help the pupils to research and create a brainstorm.

Medieval instruments:	Modern day equivalents:
STRINGS	
Box of viols – bass viol	Strings – violin, viola, cello
Medieval harp	Small harp / welsh harp / Celtic harp
Lyre	
Lute	Guitar
Rebec	Small middle-eastern violin
Medieval fiddle	Fiddle
Psaltery	Finger piano / harp
Hurdy gurdy (the main instrument in the theme tune from the TV show *Black Sails*)	

WOODWIND	
Medieval bagpipes Crumhorn Shawm Recorder Flute (transverse flute)	Bagpipes Recorder Oboe Recorder flute
BRASS	
Sacbut Cornett	Trombone Trumpet
PERCUSSION	
Tabors Nakers	Drums

A recommended website with a great range of sound samples belongs to The University of Iowa Department of Music and Theatre, on their page for *Musica Antiqua* www.music.iastate.edu/antiqua/instrument.

3.1.2 Improvisation

The keys we are most familiar with in modern music did not exist back in Medieval times. Instead musicians played in modes, surprisingly not dissimilar to jazz or folk musicians, who often still play modal music. To explain the modes, it is best to think of all of the white notes on a keyboard, with each of the 7 white notes starting its own mode, depending on the starting note. For example:

Ionian mode	CDEFGABC	Drone notes:	C – G
Dorian mode	DEFGABCD	Drone notes:	D – A
Phrygian mode	EFGABCDE	Drone notes:	E – B
Lydian mode	FGABCDEF	Drone notes:	F – C
Mixolydian mode	GABCDEFG	Drone notes:	G – D
Aeolian mode	ABCDEFGA	Drone notes:	A – E
Locrian mode	BCDEFGAB	Drone notes:	B – F

Unlike 'keys', the intervals between the scale notes in each of the modes change and so each mode has its own unique sound and character.

Activity: Improvising using modes
On a tuned percussion instrument or keyboard, choose one of the above modes and play the given drone notes, counting 4 beats for each held note. To improvise a melody, play the first note of the mode and add a rhythm. Add the 2nd and 3rd note before returning back to the first note. Gradually add each of the notes before returning to the first note each time. This pattern helps to build up the improvisation.

3.1.3 Composition
Activity 1: Medieval banquet
Compose a piece of music for a Medieval banquet. Select one of the given modes and play the notes. Use upbeat rhythms for the drone and add drums to create even more rhythmic interest. Once the accompaniment has been created, compose a tune to fit over the top. Recorders sound authentic for Medieval music.

Activity 2: Jousting tournament
Compose a piece of music for a jousting tournament. Choose one of the modes and create a very stately sounding drone and rhythm part. The melodic part must sound like a fanfare. If you have access to trumpet sounds on a keyboard or iPad then use these sounds for a more authentic effect, unless you have an actual trumpet player in the class.

Activity 3: Robin Hood
Compose a song about the legend of Robin Hood, using the story as an inspiration. Write a set of lyrics depicting one of the stories from Robin Hood. Add melody and rhythm to the lyrics and teach to a small group to perform.

3.2 MUSIC FOR KINGS AND QUEENS

1485–1600 Renaissance music:
      The Tudors and Elizabethan era
1600–1750 Baroque music

During the Renaissance and Baroque periods music was composed for royal events such as coronations. Music was also performed in the royal court for celebrations and general entertainment. Fanfares are typically associated with the announcement and entrance of royalty. A wider range of instruments became more available and composers began to compose more secular music for wider audiences. However, in order to afford making a living by playing instruments or composing, one must have been from a noble family and been supported by a patron who was often the King. During the late 16th and early 17th centuries music saw a development from modes to music composed in keys. This new style of organising notes into major and minor keys encouraged a brand-new style of music.

3.2.1 Listening
Activity 1: 'Miserere Nostri' (Thomas Tallis, 1575)
- What types of voices are singing, male or female? (*Male*)
- How many words are in this song? (*3 – Miserere, nostri, Domine*)
- Is the singing homophonic or polyphonic? (*Polyphonic*)

Activity 2: 'Flow My Tears' (John Dowland, 1596)
- Is it a male, or female voice singing and why? (*Male, castrati were popular in this era*)
- What instrument might be accompanying the voice? (*Lute*)
- What mood might a descending motif create in this type of music? (Sad or unhappy)
- Write the structure of the song, using section A and B: (A, A, B, B)

Activity 3: 'Coronation Anthem No. 1', BWV 258, 'Zadok the Priest' (George Frederik Handel, 1727)
Handel composed this piece for the coronation of King George II and it has been played at every coronation since. In addition, UEFA (European football league) have used the song since 1992 as their Champions League Anthem and so it has gained much popular notoriety:

- Do the strings play scales or arpeggios? (*Arpeggios*)
- What happens to the dynamics in the long introduction? (*Getting louder*)
- In the introduction does the pace speed up or is it kept steady? (*Kept steady*)

- When the voices enter do they sing long or short notes? (*Long*)
- What brass instrument plays along with the voices? (*Trumpet*)

Activity 4: 'Arrival of the Queen of Sheba' (Antonio Vivaldi, 1748)

This piece is from an oratorio based on the biblical stories of King Solomon with a libretto (words) taken from The First Book of Kings:

- What woodwind instrument can you hear? (*Oboe*)
- The violins play arpeggios (broken chords) over the lower strings scalic bassline. Is it an ascending or descending scale? (*Descending*)
- How many beats are in each bar? (*4 beats – crotchets*)
- In the 2012 Olympic ceremony, what fictional British hero visits the Queen to this music? (*James Bond*)

Activity 5: 'Alla Hornpipe', from *Water Music*, Suite No. 2 in D, HWV 351 (G.F. Handel, 1748)

- What woodwind instruments can you hear? (*Oboes, bassoons*)
- How many pitches do the timpani drums play? (*2*)
- What brass instrument plays when the drums enter? (*Trumpets/horns*)
- How many beats in the bar are there? (*3*)

Further listening

- 'Stabat Mater' (Palestrina, 1525–94)
- 'Ave Verum Corpus' (William Byrd, 1543–1623)
- 'Now Is the Month of Maying' (Thomas Morley, 1558–1602)
- National anthems: 'God Save the Queen'
- Hymns:
  - o 'Jerusalem' (Sir Hubert Parry, 1916),
  - o 'I Vow to Thee My Country' (Gustav Holst, 1921)
- *Pomp and Circumstance* (Marches) (Sir Edward Elgar, 1901–30)
- 'Ode to the Birthday of Queen Anne', HWV 74 (G.F. Handel, 1713) – harpsichord, solo female, slow, trumpet duets with voice
- *Suite in D for the Birthday of Prince Charles* (Michael Tippett, 1948) – starts loud, with full orchestra and gets lower; lots of imitation

- 'Crown Imperial March' (William Walton, 1937)
- Royal wedding music – music from the most recent weddings of Prince William and Prince Harry

3.2.2 Singing
Activity
Listen to recordings and learn to sing this ballad by King Henry VIII (c. 16th century): 'Pastime with Good Company', also known as the 'King's Ballad'.

3.2.3 Playing
Activity: Singing and playing: 'Greensleeves' (trad. c. 16th century)
'Greensleeves' has maintained its popularity and is well-known for being associated with King Henry VIII, although the evidence strongly suggests he did not compose it.

Lyrics:

Verse 1:
Alas, my love you do me wrong
To cast me off discourteously
And I have loved you so long
Delighting in your company

Chorus:
Greensleeves was all my joy
Greensleeves was my delight
Greensleeves was my heart of gold
And who but my Lady Greensleeves.

Practise the chord sequence in a stately tempo and if playing the chords play the chords with a flourish (one note at a time quickly in succession).

KEY Am
Verse:
Am G Am E7
Am G Am E7 Am

Chorus:
G G7 Am E7
G G7 Am E7 Am

Activity 1: 'Canon in D' (Johann Pachelbel, c. 17th century)

Part 1	F#	E	D	C#	B	A	B	C#
Part 2	D	C#	B	A	G	F#	G	E
Ground-bass	D	A	B	F#	G	D	G	A

3.2.4 Improvisation
Activity: Pachelbel's Canon
Use the ground-bass from Pachelbel's Canon and learn to play it as a class. This could be done altogether, or split into 5 groups, each group with one note. The conductor could point to each group and change the order and length of the notes. They could also have 2 notes playing at the same time. Once the ground-bass notes have been rehearsed pupils could take turns improvising over the top. To begin, pupils could choose one note and simply add rhythms, adding a 2nd or 3rd note if they feel confident.

3.2.5 Composition
Activity: Compose a royal fanfare
A fanfare is a short musical tune used to represent the introduction of someone or something important. Royalty has been introduced by trumpet fanfares through the ages as they are loud and sound very regal. Using the instruments you have available, including voices, improvise a fanfare by using only the notes – C and G. Create a strict march like pace and perhaps a drum roll underneath. Try to emulate the rhythms of a fanfare. Perhaps try adding another fanfare using the notes A and E.

Roleplay – Listen to the following fanfares and get students to enter the classroom in the roleplay of a famous king or queen. Ask the students to try to walk in a stately manner, waving to their lowly subjects:

- 'Fanfare for the Common Man' (Aaron Copland, 1942)
- 20th Century Fox Theme

3.2.6 Dancing

It was popular to dance to Pavannes and Galliards. In your class devise a stately dance to William Byrd's (c. 1590) 'Pavanne and Galliard in C', which is played by a consort of viols (early string instruments similar to violins, in different sizes).

3.3 THE BLUES

Blues songs have a history intertwined with the trans-Atlantic slave trade in the 17th–19th centuries. The style of blues music evolved from the field hollers and spirituals slaves sang while working in the plantations. The slaves brought with them many influences from African music such as vocal harmonies and strong rhythms. In contrast to the traditional and stoic hymns being sung at the American churches, the African music influences infiltrated the communities and places of worship for the communities of slaves. This developed into gospel singing, with lyrics about life and struggles, while finding hope in religion.

3.3.1 Listening activities
Activity 1: Field hollers and work songs
Watch examples of traditional field hollers on YouTube. Stand everybody in a circle and create a beat by pretending to dig with a shovel or axe. Lead a call and response using phrases about everyday life, such as, 'I'm really, really hungry', 'I've got no money', 'the dog ate my homework'. Get students to think of things that have annoyed them and use it in their field holler.

Activity 2: American negro-spirituals and gospel songs
Spirituals are the songs originally sung by negro slaves, empowering them and giving them hope of redemption; many have religious and biblical associations. Gospel songs are more specifically Christian and evangelical.

Watch the clip of the gospel song 'Oh Happy Day' (1993) from the film *Sister Act* and answer the following questions.

- Does a female or male student sing the solo? (*Male*)
- During the warm-ups, Whoopi Goldberg uses a technique called 'call and response', what does this mean? (*The leader sings, then the choir repeats*)
- What instrument is accompanying them? (*Piano*)
- The choir sings in unison at the beginning, before developing into harmonies and part-singing. Describe what unison means? (*Everyone singing the same note*)
- Do the choir stand still, or move with the music? (*Move with the music*)
- Is the style of singing strict or relaxed in style? (*Relaxed in style*)

Activity 3: 'Sweet Home Chicago'
Compare and contrast the following 2 versions of the same song – 'Sweet Home Chicago'. How has the song changed in style? Instrumentation? Dynamic? Tempo? What is kept the same in both songs? (Chord sequence, lyrics and melody)

Robert Johnson (1936)	The Blues Brothers (1978)
Solo male singer	Electric guitar
Acoustic guitar	Faster
12-bar blues	Piano
Accompaniment typically uses 2 note harmonies	Busy fills
Guitar fills	Drum-kit
	Bass guitar
	Second voice
	Brass section – trumpets and sax
	12-bar blues
	Same lyrics
	Clearer vocals

Activity 4: 'Hard Luck' (Elvis Presley, 1965)
Elvis grew up listening to blues music, before developing the style further into rock and roll by adding electronic instruments, making the tempo faster, and writing more frivolous lyrics.

YouTube: 'Hard Luck' (Elvis Presley: 1965), from the film *Hard Luck*, 1965, posted by George Corneliussen [5 May 2009]; https://youtu.be/G7Q6OlKHywA

- What instrument plays in the introduction? (*Harmonica/ mouth organ*)
- Does the harmonica play at the same time as Elvis's voice, or filling in the gaps? (*Fills*)
- What instruments join in on the second verse? (*Double bass, piano, drums*)
- What animal does Elvis sing about? (*Black cat*)

Activity 5: 'Dog House Boogie' (Seasick Steve, 2007)
YouTube clip: 'Dog House' (Seasick Steve Live on Jools Holland) [22 Jan. 2007]; https://youtu.be/pNoPNC3ebYQ

- How many strings does he have on his guitar? (*3*)
- What happens to the tempo of the song? (*Gets faster*)
- How is the percussion part added? (*Foot stomping on a box*)

3.3.2 Singing
Activity 1: Field hollers
Stand in a circle and count a steady beat of 4, stomping the right foot on beat 1 and the left foot on beat 3. Next get the pupils to pretend to dig, bending down with the shovel on beat 1 and throwing the soil over the shoulder on beat 3. Take turns to lead a call and response, singing about things that annoy you, for example, 'my little brother annoys me', 'I hate broccoli', 'homework is rubbish'.

Activity 2: Singing in parts
Two well-known songs that can be sung at the same time are: 'Swing Low Sweet Chariot' and 'When the Saints go Marching In'. Teach each song separately, then split the class in half and start one half singing one of the songs. Bring the second half of the class in to sing the second song over the top of the first. A handy hint is to sing the 'Oh' (from 'When the Saints') swiftly at the beginning of 'Swing Low'. You may need to practise or see if the children can work it out in pairs or smaller groups first depending on their ability.

Lyrics 1:
Swing low, sweet chariot,
Coming for to carry me home,
Swing low, sweet chariot,
Coming for to carry me home.

Lyrics 2:
Oh When the Saints (Oh When the Saints)
Go marching in (go marching in)
Oh When the Saints go marching in
I want to be in that number
Oh When the Saints go marching in

There is a wealth of blues songs to sing, ranging from historical songs, to contemporary blues songs. Here is a list of suggestions:

- Any songs by blues artists such as Muddy Waters, Blind Melon Jefferson, John Lee Hooker, Bessie Smith, Howlin' Wolf, Leadbelly
- *Simpsons Sings the Blues* album (1990). Any song from this album works brilliantly in schools. The track 'Moanin' Lisa Blues' works particularly well.
- *The Blues Brothers* (1980)
- 'Lean On Me' (Bill Withers, 1972)
- 'Oh Happy Day' (The Edwin Hawkins Singers, 1968)
- 'Work Song' (Nina Simone, 1961)
- 'Wade in the Water' (songwriter unknown, 1901)
- 'Swing Low, Sweet Chariot' (Wallace Willis, c. 1865)
- 'Steal Away' (Wallace Willis, c. 1862)

3.3.3 Playing
Activity 1: 12-bar blues chord structure

The blues is an excellent topic for helping young people to develop their instrumental skills. Using YouTube, type in '12-bar blues backing track in C (or G)'. The key of E works best for guitarists; however, it does mean keyboards will have to play lots of black notes and so is more complicated. Get the class to count the bars along with the video. Add on-beat claps in-between the strong beat of each bar, for example, 1 clap clap clap, 2 clap clap clap.

YouTube: Cliff Smith: C – Medium 12 Bar Blues Backing Track [10 Aug. 2018] https://youtu.be/V6aZZFnZUVk

C (C, E, G)	C	C	C
F (F, A, C)	F	C	C
G (G, B, D)	F	C	C

Chord numbers:

I	I	I	I
IV	IV	I	I
V	IV	I	I

Activity 2: St Louis Blues (W.C. Handy, 1914)

A	I hate to see de evenin' sun go down,
A	Hate to see de evenin' sun go down
B	'Cause ma baby, he done lef' dis town.

A	Feelin' tomorrow like I feel today,
A	Feel tomorrow like I feel today,
B	I'll pack my trunk, make ma git away.

C *I hate to see de*	C *evenin' sun go*	C *down,*	C
F *I hate to see de*	F *evenin' sun go*	C *down,*	C
G *'Cause ma baby,*	F *he done lef' dis*	C *town.*	C

The song lyrics fit neatly over the chords 12-bar structure.

3.3.4 Improvisation

The blues scale is the typical scale of notes used to create melodies and improvisations over the top of the 12-bar blues chord structure. Learn to play this blues scale in the key of C:

C, Eb, F, F#, G, Bb, C

To build up an improvisation get students to initially play the note C but adding their own rhythm. Next add the note Eb, then F. Most students can improvise well with these three notes. Once they have mastered this, add the next two notes, then finally Bb and C (octave higher).

3.3.5 Composition
Activity 1: Writing a blues song

After studying the lyrics from a range of blues songs, pupils can write a set of blues lyrics. The lyrics in blues songs are typically about something sad, for example when a loved one leaves. Research themes associated with the blues. A few suggestions are: sadness, hardship, unfairness, no money, no food, no life. For children at school issues might include environmental issues, family issues, social media, struggles of a teenager. Write the song lyrics using the sentence structure AAB (see 'St Louis Blues' above). After choosing a theme for the song, brainstorm words to do with that theme and then create 2 sentences; perhaps sentence A could be a problem, and sentence B could be a solution.

Activity 2

Compose a melody for your lyrics using some of the notes in the blues scale. Add swung rhythms to fit the lyrics over the 12-bar chord sequence. Play the 12-bar accompaniment. These different roles can be given to small groups in the classroom.

Activity 3: GarageBand on an iPad

Record a 12-bar blues song on GarageBand on an iPad. Follow these steps:

- Open a new project
- Extend the number of bars in your piece from 8 to 12

- Use smart drums to lay down a drum track
- Choose a guitar or keyboard smart instrument and after listening to some of the different autoplay options, choose one you like.
- Record the chords C, F and G in the order of the 12-bar blues structure.
- Repeat the chords using different instruments.
- Record the vocals using the microphone and voice recording feature.

3.3.6 Research
Research activity 1

What does the slave trade have to do with the origins of the blues?

Which American states are well-known for the blues?

What are blues lyrics typically about?

What is improvisation?

What is a walking bass?

Name 5 blues musicians and give examples of songs they wrote.

What style of rock is influenced by the blues?

Research activity 2

Research the following styles of music and write 5 characteristics about each: blues, Dixieland, rhythm 'n' blues, honkytonk, ska, rock 'n' roll, rocksteady, rockabilly

3.4 MUSIC AND WAR

Throughout the centuries music has been influenced by many different wars. Trumpet fanfares, bugle calls, military marching bands, war cries and protest songs are just some of the types of music used. During World War 1 (1914–18) music halls were popular and many songs were sung about troops coming home, and the stories of women missing their men. Many songs were comical and sing-able in nature. Dance-bands were imported from the USA and after the first UK broadcast in 1923 by Marius B. Winter they established a wide repertoire: medleys from shows, jazz, popular tin-pan alley songs, blues.

Music still plays an important role during Remembrance parades. The 'Last Post' has been a tradition since the 17th century and is a well-known bugle call played in remembrance of those who died at war.

3.4.1 Listening
Activity 1: 'Liberty Bell March' (John Philip Sousa, 1893)

- What type of ensemble is playing this march? (*Brass band*)
- Is the piece in simple (straight beats) or compound time (swung beats)? (*Swung*)
- What instrument is played to represent the Liberty Bell? (*Tubular bells*)
- What TV show was the march used on for its opening credits? (*Monty Python's Flying Circus*)

Activity 2: 'The British Grenadiers' (traditional marching song, 17th century)
Compare and contrast the following 2 versions of this famous marching song:

- Version 1: 'The British Grenadiers (remastered)' – Leonard Bernstein Conducts Great Marches [4 May 2018]; https://youtu.be/3EDQBeRx0Iw
  - Marching band / wind band
  - Snare drum introduction
  - Very loud dynamics
- Version 2: 'The British Grenadiers' – John Rutter, The Cambridge Singers [15 Oct, 2019]; https://youtu.be/YtWkCumcPvY
  - No instruments, just voices
  - SATB choir (soprano, alto, tenor, bass)
  - Vocals sing the drum parts 'pa pa pum...'
  - This version has lyrics
  - This version is quieter and softer

Activity 3: 'The Star-Spangled Banner' (Jimi Hendrix, live at Woodstock)
YouTube – Jimi Hendrix The Star-Spangled Banner American Anthem Live at Woodstock 1969, posted by Eduardo Dyablo [18 Sep. 2014]; https://youtu.be/TKAwPA14Ni4

• Watch a live video from Woodstock 1969 of Jimi Hendrix playing the American National Anthem, 'The Star-Spangled Banner'. Discuss and research whether this was, or was not, a piece of protest music for the Vietnam war?

Activity 4: *1812 Overture, Op. 49* (Pyotr Ilyich Tchaikovsky, 1880)
This overture was written in 1880 to commemorate Russia's defeat of Napoleon in 1812. It is sometimes played on events such as the American Independence Day.

• After listening to the opening of the finale, can you sing the main theme?
• How is the theme played when the first cymbals/canon shots are fired? (*Longer note values, augmentation*)
• How does the piece develop? (*A choir is added and church bells*)

Further listening: War and protest music
• 'Anarchy in the UK' (Sex Pistols) – contains many civil war references in the abbreviations and was a strong influencer of anarchy in the late 1970s.
• *War Requiem* (Benjamin Britten, 1961–2)
• 'Fanfare for the Common Man' (Aaron Copeland, 1942)
• *War Symphonies 7–9* (Dmitri Shostakovich, 1942–5)
• 'Mars – The Bringer of War', from *The Planets Suite* (Gustav Holst, 1914–16)

3.4.2 Singing
Warm-ups – 'Sound Off' military cadence by Willie Duckworth. This chant is known as the Duckworth chant. Examples can be found on YouTube.

March the pupils on the spot or moving around the classroom. The leader calls and the others respond:

Leader:	Response:
Sound-off	1–2
Sound-off	3–4
Cadence count	1–2–3–4
1–2–3–4 (altogether)	1–2–3–4

Famous marching songs from World War 1
- 'Pack Up Your Troubles in Your Old Kit Bag' (George Henry Powell, 1915)
- 'It's a Long Way to Tipperary' is an old march song from World War 1

> It's a long way to Tipperary,
> It's a long way to go.
> It's a long way to Tipperary
> To the sweetest girl I know!
> Goodbye Piccadilly,
> Farewell Leicester Square!
> It's a long way to Tipperary,
> But my heart's right there.

Famous radio songs from World War II:
- 'Boogie Woogie Bugle Boy' (The Andrews Sisters, 1941)
- 'The White Cliffs of Dover' (Vera Lynn, 1942)

Popular music songs about war or protest:
- 'Shipbuilding' (Elvis Costello, 1982)
- 'War Is Over' (John Lennon and Yoko Ono, 1972)
- 'Young, Gifted and Black' (Nina Simone, 1969)
- 'War' (The Temptations, 1969)
- 'Blowin' in the Wind' (Bob Dylan, 1963)

3.4.3 Playing
'Enola Gay' (Orchestral Manoeuvres in the Dark, 1980). This song was named after the American plane that dropped the atomic bomb on Hiroshima.

The keyboard part in this song is easy for pupils to learn and can be played as a class song because it is based on a common 4-chord sequence: C, Am, F, G

3.4.4 Improvisation
Activity: Improvise 'Sound Off' cadences
Based on the style of the military cadence create lyrics and rhythms for your own military cadences. The lyrics could be about anything topical, or nonsense lyrics. For example:

Leader:	Response:
Pizza	Pizza
Margherita	Margherita
Chicken and chips	Chicken and chips
Licketty Split	Licketty Split
1–2–3–4 (altogether)	1–2–3–4

3.4.5 Composition
Activity 1: Composing a march
Compose a piece in the style of a march. Listen to the bassline of a typical march. They tend to use note intervals of 4ths and 5ths; for example, if the march is in the key of C, C being the most important note ('tonic' note) counting up through the alphabet, notes 4 and 5 would be F and G respectively.

1	2	3	4	1	2	3	4	1	2	3	4	1	2	3	4
F	C	F	C	F	C	F	C	G	C	G	C	E	C	G	C

Try to create a drum rhythm to go over this marching bassline. Add chords too. F (F, A, C) should work well. Instruments such as a recorder or trumpet would also work well by adding a triumphant tune on top, but any instrument will do.

Activity 2: Write a protest song

As a class, brainstorm things that really annoy people. School issues could include too much homework, bullying on social media or having to wear school uniform. Global issues might include: too much plastic in the ocean, the #MeToo movement, or overcrowding in prisons. Task the pupils with a songwriting activity. In pairs, write a set of through-composed lyrics about the issue that annoys them the most. Lyrics do not have to rhyme but will have to be spoken/sung over a beat.

CHAPTER 4

Music and events

4.1 SPORTING EVENTS

4.1.1 Football music

Football chants

The largest choirs in our country happen during football matches when tens of thousands of fans sing together to support their team. The songs and chants are not written down, or taught, but picked up through oral tradition and rote learning. There are theme tunes associated with World Cups and football leagues, and each football club has their own unique song and chants. There are many clips on YouTube of fans singing at football matches.

Listening activities

Activity

'Match of the Day Theme' (Barry Stoller, 1970)

- Can you hear any background sound effects? (*Football match, fans cheering*)
- What percussion instrument can you hear? (*Drum-kit, lots of cymbals*)
- What brass instruments play the main theme, and how many are there? (*2 trumpets*)

Singing

There are numerous songs associated with football. Here is a list of songs that work well in schools:

Football chants
o 'Ole, Ole, Ole, Ole' (Spanish trad., unknown)
o 'Que Sera, Sera (Whatever Will Be Will Be)' (Doris Day, 1956)
o 'On Top of Old Smokey' (American trad., unknown; Roud folk song index 414).
o 'When the Saints Go Marching In' (unknown, 19th century)

Popular music songs:
o 'Vindaloo' (Fat Les, 2014)
o 'Waving Flag' (K'naan, 2009)
o Three Lions (Ian Brodie, Frank Skinner and David Baddiel, 1996)
o 'You'll Never Walk Alone', from *Carousel* (Rodgers and Hammerstein, 1945)

Classical music:
o 'Nessun Dorma', *from Turandot* (Giacomo Puccini, 1926)
o 'Pavane in F-sharp minor', Op. 50 (Gabrielle Faure, 1887)

Playing
Activity 1: 'When the Saints Go Marching In' (Louis Armstrong, 1959)
'When the Saints Go Marching In' is a famous jazz number sung at many sporting events. It uses the notes C – D – E – F – G and is a simple and memorable tune for all students to learn on the keyboard, xylophone, or any other tuned instrument.

G		C E F	G		C E F	G		C E F	G	E	C	E
D		E E D	C	C E G	G	F	E E F	G	E	C	D

Activity 2: Match of the Day Theme (Barry Stoller, 1970)
For a slightly more complicated tune the MOTD theme tune will definitely encourage students to work on their rhythmic skills.

Activity 3: 'Seven Nation Army' (The White Stripes, 2003)
Bass riff notes E, E, G, E, D, C, B

4.1.2 Improvisation
Activity 1
Try to create a rhythm piece based on these rhythmic sentences:

- *We are the reds and we like to eat our veg*
- *We are the blues and we never ever lose*
- *See the goal, take a kick and get it in the back of the net*
- *Ready everybody if you wanna be the best.*

Activity 2
Give each group the task of creating a football chant and get them to face another group. Then you could try to layer each of the chants.

Activity 3
Change the words of these famous songs to create a song for your own football team, or the school football team:

- 'On Top of Old Smokey'
- 'She'll Be Comin' Round the Mountain'
- 'Seven Nation Army'

4.1.3 Composition
Activity 1
Write a football song or chant for the football team at the school. Look in the *Songwriting* chapter for tips. In the lyrics include the following:

- Use the colours of the football team
- Mention the school name or location
- Write a motivational sentence to spur the team onto victory
- Write about an epic match where the football team defeated the other team
- Write about the struggles of losing a match

The best song gets to be sung by the whole class or recorded for the football team to hear and comment on.

Activity 2
Write a football chant to be used in a whole school assembly based on the call and response style to support the school football team or another local team.

4.2 RUGBY

4.2.1 Listening
Activity 1: 'World in Union' (Theme of the Rugby World Cup, 1991; lyrics by Charlie Skarbeck (1991), music by Gustav Holst (1916) 'Jupiter', from *The Planets*)

Compare and contrast

1991 Kiri Te Kanawa	2015 Paloma Faith	2019 Kiyoe Yoshioka (lead singer from the pop-rock band Ikimono-gakari)
Opera singer Harp Wind chimes Strings Electric bass Synthesiser Choir backing singers	Pop singer Piano Synthesiser Choir in background Electric drum-kit Strings	Pop/rock singer Taiko drums Gongs Strings

Activity 2: 'Swing Low, Sweet Chariot' (Willis Wallace, 1865)
Watch the 2019 version and discuss why it is a good arrangement for the Japan World Cup:

- Pentatonic scale – so has an Eastern feel
- Taiko drumming
- Lots of technology/effects on the melody
- Use of drones
- *Tremolando* (scrubbing the bow) on the strings
- Later on, bagpipes bring an element of traditionalism and fusion

Activity 3: New Zealand Haka

The New Zealand rugby team nicknamed The All Blacks perform a Haka before every rugby match they play. The performance is full of energy and expression and intended to intimidate the other team.

Watch the following YouTube clip of a performance of a Haka by the New Zealand rugby team: YouTube – England's Incredible response to an intense New Zealand Haka, posted by World Rugby [26 Oct. 2019] https://youtu.be/LgF8IVPeR48

- What is the term given for when a leader sings or speaks and everybody else repeats? (*Call and response*)
- How are the percussive sounds made? (*Stamping feet, slapping elbows and knees*)
- Does the Haka have a strong sense of beat? (*Yes*)
- Do instruments join in? (*No, it is performed a capella*)
- Other than the fierce call of the Haka words, how else do the players look and sound menacing to their opponents? (*Facial expressions, sounds with their mouths, aggressive stance, direct eye contact*)

4.2.2 Singing

- 'World in Union' (Charlie Skarbeck, 1991)
- 'Swing Low, Sweet Chariot' (Wallace Willis, c. 1865)
- 'I Vow to Thee My Country' (Sir Cecil Spring Rice, 1921; music by Gustav Holst)

Activity: Traditional All Blacks rugby team Haka

Here are the lyrics to the All Blacks Haka:

> *Ka mate! Ka mate!*
> *Ka ora! Ka ora!*
> *Ka mate! Ka mate!*
> *Ka ora! Ka ora!*
> *Tenei Te Tangata Puhuru huru*
> *Nana nei tiki mai*
> *Whakawhiti te ra*
> *A upa ne ka up ane*
> *Upane, Kaupane*
> *Whiti te ra, Hi!*

4.2.3 Playing
Activity: 'Swing Low'
Learn the notes below for the tune to the traditional song 'Swing Low'.

A, F, A, F, F, D, C
F, F, F, F, A, A, C, C

4.2.4 Improvising
Activity
Use the notes for the 'Swing Low' tune to create an improvisation. Change the notes around, just play 3 of the notes, add different rhythms. Try to make it unrecognisable. Add different types of accompaniments, drums or voices.

4.2.5 Composing
Activity: Haka
An exciting lesson for students is to get into two teams and learn to perform the traditional Haka. They can use the Haka made popular by the All Blacks rugby team, or write their own haka using words from a list of Maori vocabulary. Once the words to the haka have been chosen they should be repetitively practised with a chanting rhythm until learnt from memory. Once learnt, actions can be added. Again, these can be the similar movements to the All Blacks or totally unique. Below is a sample of some Maori vocabulary with meanings, however there are many more resources online:

* kia mau – take your stance
* Kupu – words
* Arero – tongue
* Wiri – quivering the hands
* Tinana – body
* Waiwau – spirit
* Tamanuiterá – the sun

4.3 OLYMPICS

The ancient Olympic Games celebrated events in honour of the Greek God Zeus and can be traced back to 776 BC, though continued in popularity when the Romans ceased power. The modern Olympics have continued many traditions in honour of the ancient Olympics, such as the awarding of olive wreaths for winners and the Olympic flame.

4.3.1 Opening ceremony

The opening ceremony is a festival of celebration of the host city's culture and brings together an eclectic presentation of music, dance, and theatre art from the host nation. Traditionally there is the Parade of Nations, the Olympic torch, and the singing of the Olympic hymn.

Activity 1: The Olympic Hymn (Anthem) (Spyridon Samaras, 1896)
- What instrumental family play the fanfare? (*Brass*)
- Is the choir male, female or both? (*Both*)
- Does the choir sing in homophony, or polyphony? (*Homophony*)
- Does the choir sing the same notes, or different harmonies? (*Harmonies*)
- What kind of drum plays throughout and can be heard clearly at the end of the piece? (*Timpani, kettle drums*)

Activity 2: London 2012 – Mr Bean playing 'Chariots of Fire'
Watch the clip of Mr Bean at the 2012 Olympic Games playing 'Chariots of Fire'.

- Describe the introduction – fast and loud, or quiet and slow (*Quiet and slow*)
- What instrument is Mr Bean playing? (*Keyboard*)
- What instrument plays the calls? (*French horn*)
- What instrument plays the melody? (*Piano*)
- During the performance Mr Bean gets bored. Why does he get bored? (*He is playing a repeated note*)

Activity 3: Winter Olympics – ice-skating

Listen to Ravel's (1928) 'Bolero' or watch the iconic ice-skating performance by Torvill and Dean that won them the first-ever British gold medal in the Winter Olympics in 1984.

- What type of drum can you hear?
- What family of instruments play the accompaniment?
- What type of instruments play the tune/melody?

Listen to Frank Zappa's version of the 'Bolero' on his album *The Best Band You Never Heard in Your Life*:

- Compare and contrast this to the original orchestral 'Bolero'. What differences can you hear?
- What style of music can you hear in Zappa's version?

4.3.2 Singing

Apart from the Olympic Hymn, the most popular songs from the Olympics are the national anthems (national songs, national hymn, state anthem) from all of the participating countries. Hymns are traditional and formal songs.

4.4 OTHER SPORTS

4.4.1 Listening

Cricket: 'Soul Limbo' Booker T and the MGs (1968)

- What percussion instrument can you hear first? (*Cowbell*)
- What instrument plays next? (*Piano*)
- What classic 60s sounding keyboard instrument can you hear? (*Hammond organ*)
- What part of the world does this music sound like it comes from? (*Caribbean, Latin-American*)

A great activity for children is to do the limbo dance if you have the appropriate materials.

Skiing: 'Pop Looks Bach' (Sam Fonteyn, 1980s) as heard on the TV show *Ski Sunday*

* What instrument plays first? (*Timpani drums*)
* How does the music create a feeling of going on a journey? (*The galloping rhythms, fast tempo, the melodic part is very busy and feels slightly rushed*)
* What instruments play the main theme tune? (*Violins*)
* What keyboard instrument can you hear in the background? (*Organ*)

Horseracing: 'William Tell Overture' (Gioachino Rossini, 1829)

* Describe the introduction, what instrument begins? (*Trumpet, followed by French horns and timpani drum*)
* What happens in the next section? (*The strings start very quietly, playing a tune to the giddy-up rhythm*)
* Are the dynamics terraced (in blocks), or gradual? (*Terraced – loud, quiet, loud, quiet*)

4.4.2 Playing

Motor racing: 'The Chain' (Fleetwood Mac, 1976), used for Formula 1 racing

Ideally this bass riff would be learnt on a bass guitar because of the ease of playing the riff on the bottom 2 strings – E and A. Other guitars work well too, using the same 2 strings. Otherwise the riff is easy to learn on keyboards:

A, A, B, C, B, A, G, A, B, E

4.4.3 Composing

Compose a piece of music to celebrate a future sporting event:

* Football World Cup
* Winter Olympics
* Wimbledon

4.5 CELEBRATIONS

4.5.1 Birthdays

Activity
'Happy Birthday to You' is a traditional folk song all young people will know. Therefore, it is a good resource to use to develop music skills. Split the class into 3 large groups and give each group 1 note: C, F, or G. Conduct the song by pointing your hands at the right note in the correct order it should be played.

Happy...

Birthday to you, happy		Birthday to you, happy		Birthday dear .... happy		Birthday to you.	
C	G	G	C	C	F	G	C

Create more verses by changing the lyrics to suit a school theme or celebrate qualities of the person whose birthday it is. The Polish celebration song 'Stolat, Stolat' is also a very good song to learn and is sung in the Polish language.

4.5.2 Parties
Parties are mostly filled with all different types of music. They are a great way for people to relax and unwind while catching up with friends and family, while celebrating a special occasion. Music at parties is chosen by the person hosting the party and is therefore part of their musical identity.

4.5.3 Valentine's Day: 14 February
In classical music the period between 1810 and 1900 is generally referred to as 'The Romantic' period. During this period many composers were exploring how to create mood and emotion through orchestration and tonality. Operas and symphonic poems led the way for emotive music, telling stories through the music.

4.5.4 Listening
Activity 1: *Piano Concerto No. 2 in C minor*, Op.18, 2nd movement, Adagio sostenuto (Sergei Rachmaninoff, 1900)

* What orchestral family of instruments play the introduction? (*Strings*)
* Describe the notes they play in the introduction: (*Slow, long, growing in dynamic*)
* What solo instrument enters? (*Piano*)
* What woodwind instrument plays a counter-melody? (*Clarinet*)
* Is the sense of timing strict or relaxed? (*Relaxed, rubato*)

Activity 2: Aria 'Un bel di vedremo' from the opera *Madame Butterfly* (Giacomo Puccini, 1904)

* What style of singing is this? (*Opera*)
* What instrument plays the same note as the singer? (*Harp*)
* Describe the accompaniment: (*High shimmering strings*)
* How does the aria create emotion? (*The music builds up in texture, dynamics, stronger tone, tempo, and instrumentation to create passion and drama. It then uses silence and quiet dynamics for the more reflective moment of the song*)

4.5.5 Singing
A suggested list of songs about love:

* 'Perfect' (Ed Sheeran, 2017)
* 'All of Me' (John Legend, 2013)
* 'Marry Me' (Jason Derulo, 2013)
* 'Someone Like You' (Adele, 2011)
* 'Marry You' (Bruno Mars, 2010)
* Balcony Scene from the *Romeo and Juliet* soundtrack (Craig Armstrong, 1997)
* 'I Will Always Love You' (Whitney Houston, 1992)
* 'Endless Love' (Diana Ross and Lionel Richie, 1981)
* 'All You Need is Love' (The Beatles, 1967)

See also the songs 'Shallow' and 'City of Stars' in the Musicals section of Chapter 2.

4.5.6 Weddings

There are lots of songs associated with weddings. The most recognised entrance music for the bride walking down the aisle is Richard Wagner's 'Wedding March', from his opera *Lohengrin*.

Listening

Activity 1: 'Bridal March' ('Wedding March') from the opera *Lohengrin* (Richard Wagner, 1850)
- How does the piece start? (*Trumpet fanfare*)
- Does the music feel like a march, or a waltz? (*March*)
- Is the piece in a major, or minor key? (*Major*)

Activity 2: 'Canon in D' (Johann Pachelbel, c. 17th century)
- What type of ensemble is playing this piece? (*String quartet – 2 violins, viola, cello*)
- How many notes are in the repeating ground-bass? (*8*)
- Listen to the top 3 musical layers, what do you notice? (*The parts have staggered entries and then imitate each other, showing a canonical structure*)

Traditionally music is played during the signing of the register:

'Arrival of the Queen of Sheba', from the oratorio *Solomon*, HWV 67 (G.F. Handel, 1948)
- 'Air' from *Orchestral Suite No. 3 in D major*, BWV 1068 (J.S. Bach, 1730)
- 'Wedding Day at Troldhaugen', Op. 65 (Edvard Grieg, 1897)

The most famous piece for the exit of the bride and groom is traditionally:

- 'Wedding March in C major', Op. 61 (Felix Mendelssohn, 1842)

Activity 1: Disco DJ
It is traditional to hire a music DJ to play music to celebrate a wedding by dancing at a disco. Plan your own DJ party set list to entertain an audience at a wedding. Remember to choose as many party type songs as possible.

Activity 2: DJ skills
If there is money in the budget, buy a set of DJ decks for students to practise their skills in mixing. Or, if you have access to iPads download DJ apps, for example *Traktor DJ*.

4.5.7 St Patrick's Day – 17 March
Singing
The Irish band The Dubliners are famous for modernising traditional folk songs. Here is a list of Irish songs you may find being played during St Patrick's Day celebrations:

- Danny Boy (Frederick Weatherly, 1913)
- 'Whisky in a Jar' (trad., c. 17th century)
- 'Molly Malone' (origins unknown)
- 'The Irish Rover' (trad., arranged J.M. Crofts)
- 'Finnegan's Wake' (Irish-American comic ballad, first published 1864)
- 'The Wild Rover' (Roud 1173, c. 1500)

4.6 MUSIC FESTIVALS

Music festivals are an increasingly popular phenomenon around the world where the audience listens to live music performances, as well as celebrating other arts. This topic works brilliantly in the summer term and engages pupils in cross-curricular learning.

4.6.1 Listening
Here are some of the most iconic performances from some of the most famous music festivals over time. Watch and discuss some of the performances with your class:

- Coachella, 2018 – Beyoncé
- Glastonbury, 2000 – David Bowie
- Woodstock, 1969 – Jimi Hendrix
- Newport Folk Festival, 1965 – Bob Dylan

4.6.2 Research

This is a great activity for the summer term as you can link it to local music festivals to make it more relevant.

Glastonbury Music Festival:

- Research performances from the most recent Glastonbury, or track artists performances historically.
- Print out a festival map and circle all of the stages.
- Create a list of as many music styles you can find being performed.
- Find pictures to see how the stages are set up.

Project task

As a class, in groups, pairs or individually you are going to plan a music festival. You will decide on the type of music festival and research music and artists who would be suitable for performing at your festival.

- Name the music festival – something catchy so audiences will want to find out more.
- Make a poster advertising the festival, listing some of the bands.
- Create a daytime schedule for the bands to play, considering timings for stage preparation and sound-checks.
- Draw a bird's-eye view of the stage, with the typical band set-up, making decisions on where to put instruments, amps, microphones and monitors (speakers at the front for feedback), lights.
- Draw a map of the festival showing food stalls, fairground rides etc. Be creative and imaginative. Make this out of craft materials, mod rock or clay.

4.6.3 Harvest Festival – Autumn
Singing

Harvest Festival is mostly celebrated in primary schools. To represent the celebration of the year's harvest and crops, it is tradition for young people to bring in tinned goods from home to donate to worthy causes. There are many songs that help with the festivities and are often performed in Harvest themed assemblies. Many music organisations, for example Out of the Ark, produce a range of songs to suit different abilities. Some song recommendations include:

- 'Autumn Leaves' (Joseph Kosma, 1945) (listen to the Eva Cassidy version)
- 'All Things Bright and Beautiful' (Cecil Frances Alexander, 1848)
- 'We Plough the Fields and Scatter' (Claudius Matthias, 1782)
- 'Harvest Samba' (Out of the Ark)
- 'Big Red Combine Harvester' (Out of the Ark)

4.6.4 Halloween – 31 October
Listening
Halloween music contains the following characteristics which help to create a mood of suspense and tension:

- In a minor key
- Lots of dissonance (clashing notes, semitones, e.g. E and Eb)
- 'Stab' chords, for example in the theme from *Psycho* by Bernard Herrmann
- Creepy sounding vocals, often deep male voices, or screaming ladies
- Fast rhythms that make you feel like you are being chased
- Heartbeats
- Music that swells (dynamics) or builds up tension
- Angular melodies
- Repetition of short musical ideas

Activity: *Psycho* **Theme (Bernard Herrmann, 1960)**
- What type of ensemble is playing this theme? (*String quartet – 2 violins, viola, cello*)
- How many 'stab' chords are played in the very short introduction? (*5*)
- What makes the piece feel like it is moving? (*Fast pace, chugging sound, accents*)
- Is the piece in a major or minor key? (*Minor*)

Singing
- 'Thriller' (Michael Jackson, 2008)
- 'Ghostbusters' (Ray Parker Jr, 1984)

- 'Time Warp' (Richard O'Brien, 1975)
- 'Monster Mash' (Bobby Pickett, 1962)

Improvisation
Activity: Creating tension
Choose 2 notes a semitone apart, for example E and F, or B and C. Build a composition around these 2 notes and how they relate to each other through dissonance (clashing sound). Experiment with adding 1 more note and building up in tension by using the elements of music.

Playing
Activity 1: 'Tubular Bells', Theme from *The Exorcist* (Mike Oldfield, 1973)
> E, A, E, B, E, G, A, E, C, E, D, E, B, C, E, B, E

Activity 2: 'Halloween Theme', from the film *Halloween* (John Carpenter, 1978)
> C#, F#, F#, C#, F#, F#, C#, F#, D, F#

Composition
Activity 1: Spooky sound effects
Using music programmes or apps on computers or mobile technology explore sound effects and samples. Compose a piece of music that builds tension and use the sound effects to convey the spooky atmosphere. See if you can add an element of shock or surprise.

Activity 2: Using sound recorders
Use a sound recorder app to record spooky sounds made by the class. They could be vocal noises, doors slamming, crunchy sounds, low murmuring sounds. Use these sounds to create a spooky story about trick or treating on Halloween night. For an extension write a Halloween rap and say it over the recorded sounds.

Activity 3
See Chapter 2: Storytelling – Graphic scores – Haunted house composition

4.6.5 Bonfire night – 5 November
Listening

Activity 1
On YouTube watch the New Year firework ceremony in London in 2017.

- Identify as many songs as possible.
- How many songs are recognisable?
- From what decade?

Activity 2
Watch other New Year's Eve firework displays from around the world on YouTube and discuss the styles of music used by the different countries.

Singing
- 'Firework' (Katy Perry, 2010)
- 'Rocket Man' (Elton John, 1972)
- 'Great Balls of Fire' (Jerry Lee Lewis, 1961)
- 'A Sky Full of Stars' (Coldplay, 2014)

Composition

Activity 1
Turn the *Guy Fawkes Night Rhyme* into a rap by adding a beat and rhythm to the words. Compose a backing track using samples or beatboxing.

Guy Fawkes Night Rhyme
Remember, remember the Fifth of November,
The Gunpowder Treason and Plot,
I know of no reason
Why the Gunpowder Treason
Should ever be forgot.
Guy Fawkes, Guy Fawkes, t'was his intent
To blow up the King and Parli'ment.
Three-score barrels of powder below

To prove old England's overthrow;
By God's providence he was catch'd (or by God's mercy)
With a dark lantern and burning match.
Holla boys, Holla boys, let the bells ring.
Holloa boys, holloa boys, God save the King!
And what should we do with him? Burn him!

Activity 2
Write a song about the Gunpowder Plot, or about general bonfire night traditions: Bonfire toffee; penny for a guy; bonfires; sparklers; Catherine wheels; fireworks; cinder toffee.

4.6.6 New Year's Eve – 31 December
Singing
It is traditional at midnight on New Year's Eve for everyone to gather round in a circle, cross arms over and hold the next person's hands, while singing the traditional Scottish folk song 'Auld Lang Syne' (written by Robert Burns in 1788). Young people are rarely taught this song in schools; instead they are expected to pick it up orally year after year whilst singing it during New Year's celebrations. There are some beautiful versions of the song on YouTube to use for teaching:

Burns's original Scots verse:

Verse:
Should auld acquaintance be forgot,
And never brought to mind?
Should auld acquaintance be forgot,
And auld Lang syne?

Chorus:
For auld lang syne, my jo,
For auld lang syne,
We'll tak' a cup o' kindness yet,
For auld lang syne.

4.7 RELIGIOUS FESTIVALS

4.7.1 Easter (March to April)

Listening activities

Activity 1: 'Since by Man Came Death', from *Messiah*, HWV 56 (G.F. Handel, 1741)
- Describe what happens to the dynamics in the introduction of the song. (*Quiet, then gradually grows louder*)
- Are the voices singing the same note, or different harmonies? (*Different harmonies*)
- Are the vocal parts moving together, or at different times? (*Moving together*)
- The next section of the music changes dramatically. Listen to 3 ways the music changes. (*Orchestra and organ accompaniment, major key, faster tempo, shorted notes, more attack/accentuation on the notes*)

Activity 2: 'Russian Easter Festival Overture', Op. 36 (Nikolai Rimsky-Korsakov, 1888)
- Does the piece start loudly or softly? (*Softly*)
- What family of instruments begin the first section of the piece? (*Strings*)
- After the violin solo, which instruments sound like birds fluttering? (*Flutes*)

Further listening
- *Seven Last Words from the Cross* (James MacMillan, premiered in 1994 during Holy Week)
- 'Morning Has Broken' (Eleanor Farjeon, 1931) – listen to the Cat Stevens version
- 'Lord of All Hopefulness' (Jan Struther, 1931)
- *Symphony No. 2* (*'Resurrection'*) (Gustav Mahler, 1895)
- *St Matthew Passion* (J.S. Bach, 1727)
- 'The Lord Is My Shepherd' (Francis Rous, 17th century)
- *Lamentations of Jeremiah the Prophet* (Thomas Tallis, 1565–70)

4.7.2 Vesak – Buddha Day – May/June

Vesak (or Wesak) is the most important festival in the Buddhist calendar because it is the birthday of Buddha. The Buddhist religion uses chanting and mantras to meditate bringing them more spiritually closer to Nirvana. Encourage pupils to relax and reflect by letting them take off their shoes, lie on the floor, or sit at the tables and place their head on their crossed arms. This helps students to relax their bodies and shut off immediate distractions. They are grateful for any opportunity to relax, especially in a busy school day. Chanting music can help when teaching young people how to meditate.

Listening activities

Music to use during meditation or relaxation sessions:

- *Chants of India* (Ravi Shankar, 1996, produced by George Harrison)
- Greatest Buddha Music of all Time – Buddhism Songs / Dharani / Mantra for Buddhist, Sound of Buddha, YouTube [22 May 2015] posted by Zen Moon – Relaxing Meditation videos: https://youtu.be/ABy95341Dto
- 'Vesak Sri Lanka' – YouTube [12 May 2015] posted by AnnoyboyPictures: https://youtu.be/K_G-022hvfA

Singing

Here are some famous Buddhist chants to use in the classroom:

- *Om Mani Padme Hum* – translates as 'Hail to the jewel in the lotus' and is the Compassionate Buddha
- *Om Shanti Shanti Shanti* – the Buddha chant for peace
- *Om a ra pa ca na dhih* – the Manjushri Mantra; will help to advance skills in all areas of learning. The more times it is said, the more success it is said to bring.

Improvisation

Underneath the chants it is a good idea to add a musical drone. This should be the same note, or 2 notes (generally a 5th apart, for example C – G, or A – E). Add a sense of pulse and some rhythm to give the piece a sense of movement and direction. Let the singers explore their voices and try to find the best notes to chant on. This may be affected by the pitch range of the singer.

Composition
Activity: Writing well-being chants
Set a challenge for the pupils to write their own set of chants about positive aspects of well-being. Suggestions include peace, kindness, caring, wisdom and so on.

4.7.3 Diwali – Indian Festival of Lights – Hindu/Sikh – October/November

Listening
- 'Happy Diwali' from the film *Home Delivery*
- Mukunda Mukunda from *Dashavataram*
- 'One Two Three Four' – Shahrukh Khan and Deepika Padukone, from *Channai Express*
- 'Radha' from the Bollywood movie, *Student of the Year*

4.7.4 Day of the Dead – Mexico – 31 Oct.–2 Nov.

Similar to Halloween, *Dia De Los Muertos* (Day of the Dead) celebrates the life of family and friends who have died. The idea is to celebrate their lives and therefore it is tradition to be festive by dressing up, singing, and dancing.

Listening

Activity 1: Traditional Mexican children's song – 'La Bruja' (The Witch)
Listen to Lila Downs perform 'La Bruja':

- What instruments can you hear? (*Double bass, dulcimer*)
- How many beats are in each bar? (*3*)
- A female starts singing the song solo, describe how the vocal parts change in the chorus? (*Other voices join in singing along and calling out, making sounds and whistling*)

Activity 2
Compare and contrast 2 arrangements of the Mexican song 'La Llorona':

Lila Downs (2012) 'La Llorona' (En Vivo) posted by Lila Downs [19 July 2012] (2012) https://youtu.be/oVUmQZdLAfQ	Alanna Ubach and Antonio Sol, Soundtrack to the 2017 animation *Coco*
Brass section Verse accompanied by classical guitars Jazzy Jazz bass guitar Accordion Harp Minor key	Solo voice in the intro Classical guitar Orchestral backing Faster tempo More rhythmic drum part and bass part Male duet singer

4.7.5 Hanukkah – Jewish Festival of Lights (Dec.)
Listening:
'Shalom Alechem', Barcelona Gipsy Klezmer Orchestra Live [21 June 2013] posted by BGKO: https://youtu.be/iSU0UG4VSEI

- How are the string instruments played? (*Plucked strings*)
- What wind/keyboard instrument is playing? (*Accordion*)
- What wind instrument has the tune when the tempo speeds up? (*Clarinet*)

Singing
Watch these songs on YouTube and choose whether to sing in English or in Hebrew:

- 'Hava Nagila' – traditional Israeli folk song (1915)
- Oh Hanukkah (by *Glee* cast) – with lyrics [31 Dec. 2012] posted by Chloe Bourgois https://youtu.be/HVZTl6DWAmE
- 'I Have A Little Dreidel' [19 Dec. 2011] posted by Corvettejrps: https://youtu.be/7RczPreZDFU
- 'Maoz Tzur' (Rock of Ages) – traditional song sung for Chanukah [2 Dec. 2018] posted by Hadassah Berne. https://youtu.be/4MRS5c7TbJw
- 'Shalom Chaverim' [25 Nov. 2016] posted by Dionisius Daniel: https://youtu.be/ImAIzsLUq5g

4.7.6 Guru Nanak Gurpurab – Sikh festival – 22 November
Listening

- YouTube – Guru Nanak Gurpurab Special / Audio Jukebox / Non-Stop Best Shabad Gurbani 2016 [24 Nov. 2015] posted by Sarab Sandjhi Gurbani: www.youtube.com/watch?v=pP4wbpwi6F0

4.7.7 Christmas music

Listening

Activity 1: YouTube 'Carol of the Bells' – Trans-Siberian Orchestra – Higher Quality [12 Dec. 2011] posted by J. Jay: https://youtu.be/sCabI3MdV9g
- What is the first instrument you hear? (*Guitar*)
- What traditional carol does the solo cello play in the introduction? (*'God Rest Ye Merry Gentlemen'*)
- When the loud section of the piece begins how many beats are there in each bar? (*3*)
- What wind instrument responds to the cello solo? (*Flute*)
- What percussion instrument imitates the cello tune? (*Tubular bells*)

Activity 2: 'This is Halloween' from Tim Burton's film *The Nightmare Before Christmas* (Danny Elfman, 1993)
- Describe the style of the accompaniment. (*Like a march*)
- What percussion instrument is struck on the same word? (*'This is Halloween'*)
- Describe the vocals. (*Lots of different voices, some singing, some speaking, high voices, low voices*)

Activity 3
Listen to traditional Christmas songs and write a list of seasonal words they have in common. (*Holly, bells, Santa, snow*)

Further listening
> *Christmas Oratorio,* BWV 248 (J.S. Bach, 1734)
> *Messiah,* HWV 56 (G.F. Handel, 1741)

Singing

Traditional carols
There are many traditional carols which have been sung in churches at Christmas for many years. If possible, arrange a trip for students to attend a church and listen to some carols in the venue they were composed for.

- 'The Holly and the Ivy'
- 'O Come All Ye Faithful'
- 'The First Nowell'
- 'We Three Kings'
- 'Little Drummer Boy'
- 'Silent Night' (Franz Gruber, 1818)

Modern songs
- 'Santa Tell Me' (Ariana Grande, 2013)
- 'Christmas Lights' (Coldplay, 2005)
- 'All I Want for Christmas Is You' (Mariah Carey, 1994)
- 'Merry Christmas Everyone' (Shakin' Stevens, 1991)
- 'Last Xmas' (Wham!, 1986)
- 'Christmas in Hollis' (Run DMC, 1988)
- 'Merry Christmas Everybody' (Slade, 1973)
- 'Run Run Rudolph' (Chuck Berry, 1956)
- 'Frosty the Snowman' (Walter Rollins, 1950)
- 'Rudolph the Red Nosed Reindeer' (Johnny Marks, 1949)

Songs from Christmas movies
- 'Let it Go'; 'Do You Want to Build a Snowman?', from *Frozen* (2013) and *Frozen 2* (2019)
- 'Dude, Where's My Donkey?', from *Nativity* 1–4 (2009–18)
- 'Believe'; 'Hot Chocolate', from *Polar Express* (2004)
- 'Halloween, Making Christmas', from *Nightmare Before Christmas* (1993)
- *Home Alone* (1990) Soundtrack

Playing

Activity 1: 'Jingle Bells' (James Lord Pierpont, 1857)

The most popular tune to learn on tuned instruments is 'Jingle Bells':

Jingle bells		Jingle bells		Jingle all the				way	
E	E E	E	E E	E	G	C	D	E	
C		C		C		G		C	

Oh what fun it			Is to ride on a			One horse open		Sleigh, hey!	
F	F F F	F	E	E E	E	D	D E	D	G
F			C			G		G	

Activity 2: 'Rudolph the Red Nosed Reindeer'
Chords:

> A, A, A, A,
> E, E, E, A
> A, A, A, A
> E, E, E, A
> D, A, B, E, A
> E, E, B, A

Activity 3: 'Santa Claus Is Coming to Town'
Chords:

> G, C, G, C
> G, D, G, G
> G, C, G, C
> G, D, G, C
> G, C, G, C
> A, D, A, G

Improvisation
Activity 1: Christmas rhythms
Use the rhythm for the words 'Jingle Bells' to create a piece of music. Play the rhythm on percussion, clap or use body percussion.

Using the rhythm for 'Rudolph the Red Nosed Reindeer', create a counter-rhythm.

Activity 2: Icicles
Create a piece of music using glockenspiels and xylophones. Imagine the dripping of water from an icicle. Each performer must choose one note and play it repetitively. The performer can make musical decisions about how slow or fast the drips are. Increase more icicle players to build up a group improvisation. Tell the group to think about how they start and end the piece of improvisation. Also listen to the effects of choosing different notes, for example if the players only play 2 different notes, or lots of different notes, does it work or do the sounds clash?

Composition
Activity 1: Writing Christmas songs
Writing Christmas songs is a great topic because of the variety of descriptive vocabulary and examples of Christmas songs out there to use as inspiration. Start by creating a brainstorm of seasonal words. Then see if you can find rhyming words. Next put the words into sentences and form a verse. Ideally a verse can tell or describe part of a story, and a chorus is more about the emotions involved. Once the verse and chorus has been written, use what instruments are available to create an accompaniment.

A simple chord sequence of two to three chords works well. Then hum the lyrics over the top until you settle on a tune.

Alternatively use a karaoke backing track to sing the new lyrics over and try to fit them to an already established tune.

Activity 2: Winter landscape
Compose a piece of instrumental music that creates the atmosphere of a cold and wintry day. Think about what sounds you might hear. Using instrumental resources available discuss what sounds you can create. Create a graphic score depicting the scene.

CHAPTER 5
Music and media

5.1 MUSIC AND ANIMATION

5.1.1 Listening activities

Activity 1: Cartoon themes
Play a range of cartoon themes for pupils to listen to. They have to guess which cartoons the tunes are from. It is a good idea to discuss what the pupils current favourite cartoons are and use the most relevant themes. Below are some cartoon themes that have remained popular through the recent years:

- *Gravity Falls* (2012–16) Disney Channel/Disney XD
- *Rick and Morty* (2012–present) Adult Swim
- *My Little Pony: Friendship is Magic.* Hub Network (2010)
- *Adventure Time* (2007–present) Cartoon Network
- *Phineas and Ferb* (2007–15) Disney
- *Ben 10* (2005–present)
- *Star Wars: Clone Wars.* Cartoon Network (2003)
- *SpongeBob* (1999–present)
- *Pokémon* (1997–present)
- *The Simpsons* (1989–present) Fox
- *Dragon Ball Z* (1989–96)
- *Thundercats* (1985–9 and 2011)
- *Scooby-Doo* (1969–present)
- *Tom & Jerry* (1940–present)
- *Teenage Mutant Ninja Turtles* (1987–2017)
- *Looney Toons* (1930–69)

Activity 2: 'The Sorcerer's Apprentice', from Walt Disney's *Fantasia* (Paul Dukas, 1897)
Watch the *Sorcerer's Apprentice* cartoon so that pupils understand the overall story. On the 2nd play through, stop the cartoon at key moments in the story and discuss what is happening with the music. Use elements of music prompts to encourage the use of key music vocabulary in the discussion. For example:

- The introduction – Which instruments start the piece? Is it slow or getting slower, fast or getting faster, or at a steady pace (beat)?
- How does the music change when...
- After the Sorcerer leaves what happens to the music?
- How does the music convey the build-up of water?
- What instrument plays when the Sorcerer claps his hands together?
- Describe how the music portrays the end section, when Mickey Mouse is told off by the Sorcerer.

Activity 3: Styles of music
Listen to cartoon themes from the list above and answer the suggested questions below:

- What type of ensemble is playing? orchestra, rock band, or electronic/computer music
- Instruments: Which instrument has the tune/melody? Which instrument plays in the introduction? Which is your favourite instrument?
- Describe the mood of the music – sad, happy, romantic, spooky

Further listening
   Animation: *Into the Spider-verse* (2018), *Dark Crystal* (2019); Ardman Classics – *Wallace and Gromit, Shaun the Sheep* (1989–present)
   Anime: *Spirited Away* (2001), *Dragon Ball Z* (2015–18), *Yu-Gi-Oh! GX* (2004–8); *Stitch* (2007–15)

5.1.2 Singing

Learn to sing the theme song of a popular cartoon. Here is a list of suggested songs:

- *Pokémon*
- *Scooby-Doo*
- *Ben 10*
- *SpongeBob SquarePants*
- *Garfield and Friends* (older and newer versions)
- *TMNT – Teenage Mutant Ninja Turtles*

Animation films:

- 'You're Welcome', from *Moana* (2016)
- 'Let it Go', Frozen (2013) and Frozen 2 (2019)
- 'You've Got a Friend in Me', from *Toy Story* 1–4 (1995–2019)
- 'A Whole New World', from *Aladdin* (1992)
- 'Be Our Guest', from *Beauty and the Beast* (1991)

5.1.3 Playing

There are lots of theme tunes in cartoons that are fun to learn on instruments. The themes range from easy to difficult and can be played fully on keyboards, guitars and tuned percussion. Easy to play tutorials can be found on YouTube and sheet notation can be found online:

- *The Simpsons* theme
- *Family Guy* theme
- *Scooby Doo* theme
- *SpongeBob* theme
- *Wallace and Gromit*
- *Rugrats*
- *Pokémon*

Activity

The *Scooby-Doo* theme is relatively simple for students to learn on classroom tuned percussion (glockenspiels, xylophones) and keyboards. This is because most of the notes move stepwise and there are few leaps.

Here are the letter names of the notes:

E E D D C D E A
B G E E E D C
E E D D C D E F
B G E E E D C

5.1.4 Improvisation
Activity: Sound effects

Use 1 minute from a selected cartoon and watch firstly with the sound, and then a second time in silence. Give the pupils time to choose instruments and prepare sound to illustrate the characters, mood and actions. Use the idea of free improvisation or give students specific notes to play.

5.1.5 Composition
Activity 1: Storyboards – Telling a story through music

Pupils watch a cartoon and then draw a storyboard of the cartoon using a blank storyboard resource. By breaking down the story and discussing what happens and the mood of each section, pupils are able to describe how they could use music to illustrate each section. This task could be done as a whole class if each table/group is given a different scene in the storyboard to portray through music.

Activity 2: GarageBand

Upload a cartoon clip and use a computer programme such as GarageBand to compose music to the given clip. Pupils can add music samples, or sequence their own music using a midi keyboard. The idea is for pupils to match the sounds with the timeline of the cartoon. There is a wide range of sound effects on most music programmes for pupils to use.

Activity 3: Stop-frame animation

Using iPads, download a stop-frame animation app. Create characters and backgrounds of your favourite cartoons, or tell children to bring in their own small character toys. Lego works well (the Lego Star Wars calendar provides miniature Star Wars Lego) to use in short animations. Once the stop-frame animation has been made, upload it to YouTube and then compose music to go over the top of the animation.

5.2 FILM MUSIC

5.2.1 Listening

Activity 1: Guess the film themes
Play a range of famous film themes for students to listen to and put in the correct order:

Star Wars, Superman, Jurassic Park, Indiana Jones, Home Alone, Jaws, Marvel Avengers, Ghostbusters, Harry Potter, Mission Impossible, Back to the Future

Activity 2: Film genre
Brainstorm films for different film genres (see the table below). Think of films associated with different film genres and the words associated with the film genre. Finally discuss what the music may sound like for the film genre. At this point discuss mood, instrumentation, style of music, sound effects etc. Play a typical example of music to represent the genre, some examples are given in the table below.

Film genre (suggested piece to play)	Film titles	Words associated with the genre	Music characteristics
WESTERN *The Good, the Bad, and the Ugly*, Ennio Morricone	*Rango, Back to the Future III, The Good the Bad and The Ugly*	Cowboys, desert, cactus, gunslingers, lasso, Wild West	Vocal chanting, whistles, tribal drumming, rhythms representing galloping horses or speeding trains
SCI-FI *Tron Legacy Soundtrack*, DaftPunk	*Star Wars, Tron, Men in Black, Independence Day, Ready Player One, Stranger Things*	Space, aliens, futuristic, technology	Electronic/computer music, atmospheric, ambience, looping sounds

HORROR (Psycho, shower scene music)	Jaws, Goosebumps, Hotel Transylvania, Gremlins, Paranorman, A Nightmare Before Christmas	Scary, ghosts, blood, spooky	Clashing notes Stabbing chords Psycho, shower scene music
ROMANTIC (*Titanic* theme, Celine Dion)	Titanic, La La Land, Gnomeo and Juliet, Aladdin, Frozen	Love, heart, romance, kiss, happy	Slow, flute, harps, long tunes, major key, swooping melodies
ACTION (*Indiana Jones* theme, John Williams)	Marvel films: Guardians of the Galaxy, Infinity Wars. Transformers, Indiana Jones, Fast and Furious, Tomb Raider, The Mummy	Car chase, adventure, fighting, suspense, action	Fast, loud, heroic themes, Full orchestra, brass/ trumpets

Activity 3: The Good, the Bad and the Ugly Theme (Ennio Morricone, 1966)

- Describe the first instrument to play and its role. (*It sounds like tribal drums, setting the tempo*)
- What effect does the 'giddy-up' sounding rhythm have on the piece? (*It sounds like horses galloping, movement, a journey*)
- Describe the vocals over the electric guitar tune (*Tribal chanting, then singing long notes*)
- What sound effect can you hear when the 2 trumpets play? (*Guns shooting*)

Activity 4: 'Tubular Bells', Theme from *The Exorcist* (Mike Oldfield, 1973)

- What instrument is playing the riff? (*Bass guitar*)
- Is there a melody or a repeating musical idea? (*Repeating musical idea*)

- What is the time signature? Does it change between 7/4 and 4/4, or 5/4 and 4/4? (*7/4 and 4/4*)
- What is the tonality of this piece? (*Minor*)
- Why might this music suit a horror film? (*Stabbing chords, chasing feel*)
- Why do you think the chords are given the term 'stabbing chords'? Why do you think Oldfield used this effect for his music? (*Orchestral hits to add contrast and create a sense of uncertainty*)
- How does Oldfield achieve a minimalist effect with the keyboard riff? (constant repetition; the beat feels unpredictable)

5.2.2 Singing

There are lots of songs associated with films:

- Animations such as *Jungle Book, Lion King, Frozen, Cars*
- Musicals such as *Oliver Twist, Mary Poppins, The Greatest Showman Pitch Perfect, High School Musical*

5.2.3 Playing

There are lots of theme tunes in films that range from easy to difficult, to learn on tuned instruments:

- *Indiana Jones* theme
- *Superman* theme
- *Star Wars* theme
- 'Imperial March', from *Star Wars*
- *Mission Impossible*
- *Harry Potter* theme

5.2.4 Composition
Activity 1: Using film clips

Choose a film clip for the pupils to compose a piece of music to. The music can be composed on any available instruments or technology, but must illustrate the mood, characters and story. Pupils should try to explain how they have created their piece of music and why they feel it represents the given film clip.

Activity 2: Building tension

Compose a piece of music for a spooky horror film by exploring how to create tension. Look at the musical elements and how they can be used to build up the music:

- tempo – getting faster
- dynamics – getting louder
- pitch – getting higher
- texture – getting thicker, more parts being added

Activity 3: Sound effects

Discuss what kind of sound effects you can hear in films. How do you think they are made? Think about how to make homemade sound effects, for example, doors slamming, footsteps, shakers for rain. Use a video clip to add sound effects over.

5.3 COMPUTER GAME MUSIC

Computer gaming is a popular past-time for young people. The most common devices used to play computer games are currently: Xbox; PlayStation; Nintendo Switch; Nintendo Wii; PC; smart phones and iPads, otherwise known as 'mobile technology'. Pupils are generally interested in learning about the history of computer game music and recognise it as an important genre of music.

5.3.1 History of game music

- Video games emerged as a form of entertainment in the 1970s.
- Music was only possible on arcade games to begin with and was monophonic (one line of sound/tune) for example, Pacman.
- The popular Atari 2600 could generate two tones (two musical lines happening at the same time – a melody and bassline), and took steps towards 'sampled sounds', which are sounds and instruments recorded directly into the computer instead of computer-generated sounds.

- Composers were limited in terms of polyphony (the number of notes that could be played at one time). Only 3 notes could be played simultaneously on the Nintendo Entertainment System. A great deal of effort was put into creating the illusion that more notes are playing.
- Throughout the years, technological developments in multimedia meant that more tones could be added.
- First-ever concert of computer game music – *Dragon Quest* (family concert) held on 20 August 1987 at Suntory Hall, Tokyo, Japan.

5.3.2 Listening activities
Activity 1: The history of computer game music
Play 4 or more computer themes and get pupils to place them in chronological order. Discuss what it was about the music that helped them to choose that order.

- Original Mario theme, 'Ground Theme' or 'Overworld Theme' (Koji Kondo, 1985)
- Sonic the Hedgehog Theme (Masato Nakamura, 1991)
- Tetris theme 'Type A' from Nintendo Gameboy (Hirokazu Tanaka, 1989)

Activity 2: 'Volume Alpha', C418, Minecraft theme (Daniel Rosenfeld, 2011)
- What 5-note scale is the Minecraft theme based around? (*Pentatonic*)
- Is the theme loud and fast, or soft and slow? (*Soft and slow*)
- Does the music sound improvised or composed? (*Improvised*)

Activity 3
Listen to the following pieces of computer game music and circle the words you think best describes the music:

Circle the words: Exciting, dramatic, tuneful, low, high, fast, slow, strings, brass, drums, loud, quiet

Piece 1	'Liberi Fatali', from *The Final Fantasy Series* (Nobuo Uematsu, 1999)
Piece 2	'Nate's Theme', from *Uncharted* (Greg Edmondson, 2007)
Piece 3	Theme from *Killzone 2* (Joris De Man, 2009)
Piece 4	'Cloud Surfing' from *Enslaved* (Nitin Sawhney, 2010)

Activity 4

Use this YouTube clip to demonstrate the development in sound and therefore technology. It traces the development from 1985 to 2018:

YouTube – Evolution of Super Mario Bros. Theme Song (1985–2018) posted by Shiromi [29 Aug. 2018] https://youtu.be/iEHgX_h8lYU

Other popular computer games with theme music to listen to:

- FNAF – Five Nights at Freddie's
- Terraria
- Plants Vs Zombies
- Lego computer game franchise
- Subnautica
- Sea of Thieves enables players to choose from 4 instruments – hurdy-gurdy, banjo, drums, xylophone – and make music together that fit the theme of sea shanties and jigs.
- Rayman's iPad app

5.3.3 Singing

There are not many songs associated with computer games as the music is generally instrumental, due to being able to concentrate during gameplay. Parodies are very popular. JT Machinima is a group of popular songwriters of computer game parodies and many of their songs are known to young people, for example 'Five Long Nights' and 'Join Us for a Bite' from the game *FNAF*. Other Youtubers write their own parodies, for example, Captain Sparklez wrote *T.N.T.* Many children know these parodies through watching YouTube and subscribing to the composers of this style of song. Roblox is also a popular community platform game where users can join in virtual discos.

5.3.4 Playing

Suggestions for computer themes to play on tuned instruments are:

- *Angry Birds*
- *Minecraft* – pentatonic scale (all five black notes on a keyboard)
- *Tetris* based on an old Russian folk song called 'Korobeiniki' dating back to 1861.
- *Mario Bros* (although there is a lot of syncopation so it can be tricky to learn)

5.3.5 Improvisation
Activity

Watch a level of a computer game and improvise music to play along with the computer game. Choose a theme or instrument to represent different characters, scenes, or props. Think about utilising the characteristics of computer game music:

- Typically, songs that are designed to loop indefinitely, rather than lasting a set amount of time with an arranged ending or fading.
- Music designed to create atmosphere, mood and tension. A similar purpose to film music.
- Pieces that are memorable, so they stay on people's minds, therefore urging them to play the computer game.

5.3.6 Composition
Activity 1: Mood and characterisation

Use a well-known platform computer game such as *Mario Brothers*, or *Sonic the Hedgehog*. Identify and listen to the main character theme. Describe the qualities of the theme (heroic, happy, exciting, action). Identify and listen to the music that represents the end of level 'baddie'. Describe the qualities of the theme (dangerous, something's going to happen, watch out).

Create a storyboard to represent a level from the game. Each group of pupils could compose music to illustrate the section of the game level. For example, one student could recreate the jump sounds with their voice/instrument. Another group could create music to represent the climbing action, or swimming action. This would be an easier task using technology, however, can also be a composition task for acoustic instruments.

Activity 2: *Fortnite* remixes
The computer game *Fortnite* has had extreme amounts of success, as well as hosting the largest ever virtual concert in February 2019 by EDM artist Marshmello. *Fortnite* currently has up to 10.8 million users and is a global platform for communication. The lobby music from *Fortnite* is very atmospheric and creates an element of tension before players start their game. There have been remixes made of this lobby music.

The player's character can be made to dance – emotes – many of which can be found on YouTube. Some popular emotes are: infinite dab, orange justice, llama bell, the floss. Try to create a remix using different music from the emotes. Listen to a variety of emote music and make musical decisions about which would sound good in a mix together. Adapt the tempo and tonality to increase the potential success of the mix. Create a structured dance using some of the dance moves from the emotes.

Activity 3: Looping musical ideas (see also the Minimalism section in Chapter 7)
Use the idea of composing short musical ideas (choose several notes) and looping them to create a longer piece of music. Experiment changing the musical idea by exploring how the elements of music can affect the sound.

Pupils should compose short, repetitive sections of music to illustrate certain aspects of your chosen computer game. Write a brief explanation of how and why you have composed music for each particular section (use words such as tempo, dynamics, pitch, rhythm, instrumentation, sound effects, layering/texture, structure, harmony, loop, riff).

5.4 MUSIC AND ADVERTS

Music and adverts suit more of a secondary school theme as it can be linked to business studies with topics such as advertising, marketing and consumerism. It is an important topic because it highlights the importance of using a short musical idea, as a hook, to stay in a person's musical memory. This is a key feature of teaching composition as fundamental steps of composition teaching are about the creation of a short musical idea, and how to utilise repetition.

Many young people experience adverts on the internet using sites such as YouTube. The cinema is another place where they may experience adverts. Adverts selling fast food, toys, technology or cars are the types most young people may be aware of.

5.4.1 Listening activities
Activity 1: TV and radio adverts
Play a selection of current adverts and discuss the following:

- What is an advert?
- Who is the advert aimed at? Market?
- How does the advert sell the product? Discuss:
- The soundtrack (use music, voice-overs, silence, sound effects, jingles, hooks) / comedy / props to sell the product?
- The visuals – location/setting, props, actors, costumes/fashion
- The storyboard?

Activity 2: Hooks
A hook is a short musical idea lasting only a few notes long. It is easily recognisable and memorable due to repetition either within the advert, or during consistent use in adverts associated with the product over the years, for example, the *McDonalds* hook, 'I'm Lovin it', (accompanied by added whistle notes). The hook is always the last thing to be played at the end of the advert, with the purpose of sticking in someone's mind.

- Go Compare – Count how many times you hear the product being sung? Why does the song stick in your memory?

Ask pupils which adverts have stuck in their minds because of the musical hook at the end of the advert? Watch the adverts on YouTube and see why the advert is memorable.

The following adverts all have short recognisable hooks at the end:

- McDonalds – 'I'm lovin' it'
- Tesco – 'Every little helps'
- KFC – 'Finger lickin' good'
- Skittles – 'Taste the rainbow
- Calgon – 'Washing machines live longer with Calgon'
- Webuyanycar.com – 'We buy any car, dot com'
- Penguin – 'P-p-p-pick up a Penguin'

Activity 3: Jingles
Jingles have the same function as hooks, they are put in adverts to stick in people's heads. However, jingles are longer than hooks and are more similar to a tune:

- 'Toys R Us' theme song
- 'Coca-cola' Christmas advert – Holidays Are Coming
- 'R Whites Lemonade' advert song

5.4.2 Singing
Singing songs from adverts often depends what adverts are popular at the current time. The 'Toys R Us' theme is a great song, but unfortunately will probably lose popularity over time. John Lewis has provided a wealth of singing repertoire associated with its adverts, in particular the Christmas adverts, for example:

- 'Golden Slumbers' (The Beatles, 1969) – sung by Elbow in 2017
- 'Half the World Away' (Oasis, 1994) – sung by Aurora in 2015
- 'Somewhere Only We Know' (Keane, 2004) – sung by Lily Allen in 2013
- 'The Power of Love' (Frankie Goes to Hollywood, 1984) – sung by Gabrielle Aplin in 2012
- 'Your Song' (Elton John, 1970) – sung by Ellie Goulding in 2010
- 'Sweet Child O' Mine' (Guns N' Roses, 1987) – sung by Taken by Trees in 2009

5.4.3 Playing
Activity

Write the notes for several advert hooks on a piece of paper and ask students to play the notes on a tuned instrument to work out what advert the jingle/hook is from. For example:

- GGEDC – Asda
- EDCC – 'I'm Lovin' It' – McDonalds
- EGC – Go Compare

5.4.4 Improvisation
Activity

Take one hook, for example the McDonalds hook 'I'm lovin' it' and use the notes to improvise a 1-minute piece of music. Ideas for improvisation are:

- Repeat the notes in the same order as slowly as possible
- Change the order of the notes, either freely, or pre-planned
- Use the notes to create rhythms and tunes

5.4.5 Composition
Activity 1: Using a hook or jingle to compose music

Use an advert hook or jingle to compose a piece of music. Develop the composition by:

- Adding chords underneath
- Adding lyrics and turning the hook or jingle into a song based on the advert product
- Adapting the melody
- Exploring different instrumentation

Activity 2: Making your own advert
- Choose a product to sell in an advert
- Write a script for the voiceover
- Draw a short storyboard of what happens in the advert
- Compose and record a piece of music for the advert

- Record the voiceover.
- If you have access to an iPad, use the camera to film the advert. iMovie is a suitable app to edit the film footage. Add the music over the edited advert.
- Share the finished adverts with the class.

CHAPTER 6
Modern music

6.1 JAZZ MUSIC

Just before the turn of the century in New Orleans, USA, a new style of music began being played in bars, mostly in the black urban areas. This new style had derived from the blues style, yet had faster rhythms, tempo and more energy. The big band (dance band) era began in the 1920s, fusing this new contemporary style with traditional dances like foxtrot and tango. Dance bands became popular in England too playing jazz standards in dance halls and clubs. The opera *Porgy and Bess* (1935) written by George and Ira Gershwin, and musical *West Side Story* (1961) with music by Leonard Bernstein, fused elements of classical music and jazz, bringing the jazz style to an even wider new audience. Jazz is an eclectic mix of many styles yet ultimately can be recognised by the swing rhythms, jazz harmonies, instrumentation and solo improvisations.

6.1.1 Listening activities
Great jazz artists and suggested listening:

Trumpet
o Louis Armstrong (1901–71) 'What a Wonderful World', 'West End Blues', 'Potato Head Blues', 'Heebie Jeebies', 'Cornet Chop Suey'
o Miles Davis (1926–91) 'So What', 'Summertime' from *Porgy and Bess*

Piano
o William 'Count' Basie (1904–84) 'Swingin' The Blues', 'One O' Clock Jump', 'Good Morning Blues'

- Duke Ellington (1899–1974) 'Take the A-Train', 'In a Sentimental Mood'
- Ray Charles (1930–2004) 'Hit the Road Jack', 'Georgia on My Mind'
- Dave Brubeck (1920–2012) 'Take Five', 'Blue Rondo a la Turk', 'Unsquare Dance'
- Oscar Peterson (1925–2007) 'Night Train'
- Thelonius Monk (1917–82) 'Round Midnight'

Guitar
- Django Reinhardt (1910–53) 'Minor Swing', 'Brazil'

Clarinet
- Benny Goodman ('The King of Swing') (1909–86) 'Sing, Sing, Sing'
- Acker Bilk (1929–2014) 'Stranger on the Shore'

Saxophone
- Charlie (Bird) Parker (1920–55) 'Yardbird Suite', 'Billie's Bounce'
- John Coltrane (1926–67) 'Countdown', 'Giant Steps', 'On Green Dolphin Street'
- Stan Getz (1927–91) 'Girl from Ipanema'

Violin
- Stephane Grappelli (1908–97) 'Minor Swing'

Activity 1
Listen to any of the songs suggested above and answer the following general questions:

- What instruments can you hear?
- What mood does the piece create?
- Is the piece fast or slow?
- Is the piece for dancing?
- What picture do you have in your mind when you listen to this song?
- What style of jazz is this?

For younger children, print out a selection of instruments typically used for jazz music – trumpet, saxophone, piano, harmonica/mouth organ, double bass, jazz drum kit with brushes, trombone, clarinet, violin, bass guitar.

Activity 2

Listen to a recording of 'Take Five' (1959) by Dave Brubeck and answer the following questions:

- What is the first instrument to play? (*Drums*)
- Which is the second instrument to play and what does it play? (*Piano chords and bass notes*)
- Name the instrument that plays the tune: (*Saxophone*)
- How many beats are in each bar? (*5*)
- Can you tap the timing of the rhythm?

Activity 3

Glenn Miller (1939) 'In the Mood'

Listen to the songs and note down the structure of the song using sections A, B, C, D etc.

- Are the rhythms straight or swung (dotted)? (*Swung*)
- One minute into the song what instrument has the first solo call? (*Saxophone*) And what other solo instrument responds? (*Saxophone*)
- Do the music solos sounds pre-composed, or improvised? (*Improvised*)
- Does the main tune (referred to as 'the Head', as in 'back to the Head) sound pre-composed or improvised? (*Pre-composed*)
- What type of bass instrument is it? (*Double bass*) Describe the role of the bass? (*Walking bass*)

6.1.2 Singing
Activity: Scat singing warm-ups

Scat singing was popular in the early 20th century and first performed by jazz singers. Scat singing is the improvisatory style of singing where nonsense words are used to express a sense of musical freedom. Watch a YouTube video of Louis Armstrong performing scat singing, for instance in his 1927 song 'Hotter Than That'. Notably the scat singing style was made famous by Louis Armstrong who is said to have forgotten his words and sang random syllables instead.

Scat singing works well as a vocal warm-up game, especially when using call and response. Starting simple at first, then building up the number of syllables:

Teacher 'Bah, bah, bah'
Children 'Bah, bah, bah'
Teacher 'Do-be-do'
Children 'Do-be-do'
Teacher 'Do-be-do-be-do-wah'
Children 'Do-be-do-be-do-wah'
Teacher 'Sha-la-la-bop-de-do'
Children 'Sha-la-la-bop-de-do'
Teacher 'Ding-a-lang-zing-zoom'
Children 'Ding-a-lang-zing-zoom'
Teacher 'Shoop-shoop-bop-da-do'
Children 'Shoop-shoop-bop-da-do'

Get everyone around in a circle and take turns to improvise some nonsense words.

Songs:
Great jazz songs to learn with students are as follows:

- 'When the Saints Go Marching In' (Louis Armstrong, 1938)
- 'Fever' (Peggy Lee, 1956)
- 'Stormy Weather' (Harold Arlen, 1933)
- 'Fly Me to the Moon' (Bart Howard, 1954)
- 'I Got Rhythm' and 'Summertime' (George and Ira Gershwin, 1930, 1934)

6.1.3 Playing
Activity: Learn the bassline of 'Chameleon' (Herbie Hancock, 1973)

1 2 3 + 4 +	1 2 3 + 4 +	1 2 3 4	1 2 3 4
G G# A	A# G# A# C C# D	D# C# D#	

These jazz numbers have playable bass-lines or tunes:

* 'When the Saints Go Marching In'
* 'Fever', Peggy Lee – has an iconic bass riff played over onbeat finger clicks.
* 'Tequila' (The Champs, 1958)
* 'Lullaby of Birdland' (George Shearing, 1952)

6.1.4 Improvisation
Activity
In jazz, musicians often use the blues scale (see Chapter 3 – The blues) or the pentatonic scale to improvise. Start using one note only, and add a swung (dotted) rhythm. Next add a second note. Have a musical conversation with the students, asking a question (by playing an improvised rhythmic pattern on up to three notes), which they then have to answer.

Explore these techniques of jazz playing to develop your jazz style of improvisation further:

* Syncopation
* Sequence
* Imitation
* Repetition/echo

6.1.5 Composition
Activity 1: Scat song
Write and compose your own scat song. Get students to do a brainstorm of all scat/nonsense syllables. In the style of the vocal group Pentatonix, add a bassline and accompaniment using voices.

Activity 2: Blues scale – composing a bass riff
Using the notes of the blues scale create a bass riff that is short, simple and easy to remember. Try to make sure it has a swung/dotted rhythm.

Activity 3: Explore walking bass

Use an existing walking bass as inspiration to compose, for example, the walking bass in 'Fly Me to the Moon'. Start the walking bass on the tonic note of the key, for example if your piece has the note C as the tonal centre (note C is the most important), start the walking bass on note C, and finish it on note C. It must play strictly on the beat.

Research activity

Adolphe Sax was the inventor of the saxophone and led a very dramatic life, nearly dying 9 times. His life-story is one of overcoming the odds to be very successful and makes an interesting case study for research.

6.2 MODERN MUSIC STYLES

All music is popular to somebody and so the term is often misrepresented. 'Pop' music as we know it, is the result of music becoming more popularised after the Second World War. It coincided with the technological developments which enabled a wider audience to listen to and be able to make music themselves. The ability to record music became more affordable and available, influencing more people to develop a musical identity. With the emergence of more technologies being more readily accessible people's access became greater. Blues music had influenced both jazz and rock and roll music, paving the way forward for hundreds of modern music genre to emerge over future decades.

A Timeline of some modern music styles:

Decade	50s	60s	70s	80s	90s	00s	10s
'Pop' styles	Rock and roll	Beatnik	Disco	New Wave	Britpop Boy bands Girl bands	Chart	K-pop
Other styles	Standards Jazz Country Blues	R&B Psychedelia Folk	Prog. rock Punk Reggae	Glam rock Stadium rock	Grunge R'n'b Hip-hop	Garage Emo MCing Fusions	Grime Drill

6.2.1 Listening
Activity 1: Recognising popular music genre
The pop music repertoire is forever growing as more music is popular in the charts and online streaming is more readily accessible. There are some popular classic songs which remain well-known across many generations. Play pieces of music from different styles to the class. Generate discussions about the different styles of music. Do pupils notice any stylistic characteristics of the music which determines its genre type?

Activity 2: Guess the pop artist
Play famous pop songs by the following artists and ask pupils to guess the track name and artist:

Michael Jackson, Kylie Minogue, One Direction, Katy Perry, Ed Sheeran, Little Mix, Justin Bieber, Ariana Grande, Taylor Swift, Lady Gaga, Adele, Justin Timberlake, Beyoncé, Jay-Z, Eminem.

Activity 3: Guess the style
Play music from a range of popular music styles. Print out picture cards or write the styles out on small pieces of card. The students have to list the correct styles of music in the order they hear the music being played. Choose from the following styles depending on your class age: boy/girl-band; rock; pop; disco; punk; jazz; grime; club dance; rock and roll. Add a wider variety of styles if you want: opera, classical, African drumming; Indian fusion.

6.3 1950s

6.3.1 Research questions for class

- When did rock and roll begin?
- Can you name 4 rock and roll singers and 4 rock and roll bands?
- What musical characteristics define rock and roll music?
- What are typical rock and roll instruments?
- What kind of fashion did people wear during the rock and roll years?
- Who was known as the king of rock and roll?

6.3.2 Listening
Activity 1: Elvis, Chuck and Little Richard

Put three pictures on the board of Elvis Presley, Chuck Berry and Little Richard. Play the class a mixture of songs by each artist and ask them to guess who has recorded each song, writing the name of the song under the correct artist. Song examples are: 'Jailhouse Rock'; 'Johnny B. Goode'; 'Heartbreak Hotel'; 'Blue Suede Shoes'; 'Maybelline'; 'Roll Over Beethoven'; 'Tutti Frutti'; 'Long Tall Sally'.

Activity 2: 'Roll Over Beethoven'

Listen to 2 versions of the song 'Roll Over Beethoven', first by Chuck Berry (1956), then by The Beatles (1963). Compare the two songs to find similarities and differences.

6.3.3 Singing

Most songs by Elvis Presley (1935–77) or Chuck Berry (1926–2017) work well with classes as they are fun, full of energy, have simple lyrics and chords.

Suggested songs:

- Elvis Presley – 'Hound Dog', 'Jailhouse Rock', 'Suspicious Minds', 'Always on My Mind', 'Blue Suede Shoes', 'My Way', 'Heartbreak Hotel', 'Love Me Tender'
- Chuck Berry – 'Maybelline', 'Run Run Rudolph', 'Johnny B. Goode', 'Rock and Roll Music', 'Roll Over Beethoven'
- Jerry Lee Lewis (1957) 'Great Balls of Fire'
- Little Richard (1955) 'Tutti Frutti'
- Buddy Holly (1958) 'That'll Be the Day'
- Bill Haley (1952) 'Rock Around the Clock'
- Joe Turner (1954) 'Shake, Rattle and Roll'
- The Coasters (1958) 'Yakety Yak'
- Drifters (1959) 'There Goes My Baby'

6.3.4 Playing
Activity: 'Hound Dog' (Elvis Presley, 1956)

Elvis Presley's version of 'Hound Dog' (originally recorded by Big Mama Thornton in 1952) has a great bassline for students to learn as it is based on the 12 bar blues chord sequence and is simply played as broken chords. The lyrics follow the blues lyrics structure with the sentences being AAB. The chord sequence is simple to learn and works well in the classroom.

'Hound Dog' *chords:*

C, C, C, C,
F, F, C, C,
G, F, C, C

6.4 1960s

6.4.1 Research questions for class

Ask the class to name 5 songs by The Beatles.

Ask the class if they can name the four members of The Beatles (*John Lennon, Paul McCartney, George Harrison, Ringo Starr*).

The 1960s was dominated by The Beatles, who were massively popular around the world until they went their separate ways in 1970 after becoming much more experimental. Psychedelia and progressive rock embraced more experimental techniques and bands had more creative licence over their music. In the USA the West Coast saw a dominance of surf rock led by bands like The Beach Boys, while Tamla Motown in Detroit had the following artists on their records: Diana Ross and The Supremes, Jackson 5, Stevie Wonder, Marvin Gaye, Aretha Franklin.

6.4.2 Listening
'Love Me Do' (The Beatles, 1962)

- Describe the instrumentation (2 *vocals, bass guitar, electric and acoustic guitar, tambourine, cymbal*)
- Which instrument gives the piece a bluesy feel? (*Harmonica*)
- How many chords are used in this song? (2)
- Write down the structure of the song: (*Instrumental, verse, verse, bridge, verse, instrumental version of bridge, verse.*)

'Ticket to Ride' (The Beatles 1965)
- The first chord is held for a long time, on which word does it change? (*Away*)
- Describe the tempo (*Moderate*)
- Describe the instrumentation (*Vocals – echo effect, electric guitar, bass guitar, tambourine*)
- What happens to the tempo at the end of the song? (*Speeds up*)

Surfin' USA (Beach Boys, 1963)
- Describe the introduction (*Hawaiian guitar solo*)
- What instrument accompanies the singing in the verse? (*Drums*)
- What words do the backing singers sing in the chorus? (*'Inside, outside, USA'*)
- What keyboard instrument can you hear, especially in the instrumental middle 8 section? (*Hammond organ*)

'California Dreaming' (Mamas and Papas, 1966)
- What instrument plays the introduction? (*2 acoustic guitars*)
- How is the instrument played, chords, or picking (plucking strings)? (*Picking/plucking strings*)
- Describe the vocal parts (*Solo singer calls, and the backing singers respond by repeating the lyrics, but singing different melodies and in harmonies*)

Further listening
- 'For Once in My Life' (Stevie Wonder, 1968)
- 'Voodoo Child' (Jimi Hendrix, 1968)
- 'Light My Fire' (The Doors, 1967)
- 'Respect' (Aretha Franklin, 1967)
- 'House of the Rising Sun' (The Animals, 1964)
- 'Baby Love' (The Supremes, 1964)

6.4.3 Playing
Activity 1: Eleanor Rigby (The Beatles, 1966)
'Eleanor Rigby' uses two chords – E minor (E, G, B) and C major (C, E, G). Therefore it is quite easy for the class to play on tuned instruments.

6.5 1970s

6.5.1 Research questions for class

Brainstorm a list of bands and songs from the decade of the 1970s.

What styles were prominent in this decade?

In the 1970s many different styles of rock emerged, folk rock, progressive rock and punk rock being culturally important. The commercial market started to incorporate university students and became anti-pop. This led to many protest and anti-establishment songs. Reggae became increasingly popular too (see Chapter 8: Global music – Latin-America – Reggae).

Tamla Motown was producing many soul artists and records. Soul is a musical style that combines elements of gospel music, and rhythm and blues. Soul would be played at the local discos along with disco classics such as 'D.I.S.C.O.', 'Saturday Night Fever' and 'Y.M.C.A.'.

By the 1970s the first heavy metal bands had already formed both in the USA and Britain. Led Zeppelin, Black Sabbath and Deep Purple were among the bands selling out stadiums. The musical characteristics of heavy metal include loud, energetic drum parts, thumping basslines, distorted power chords on electric guitar, and virtuosic, powerful lead guitar solos. The singer often sings in a screeching or barking style. The lyrics are mostly about topics such as rebellion and violence.

6.5.2 Listening

Activity 1: 'A.B.C.' (Jackson 5, 1970)

- What does the singer sing in the introduction? (*Ba ba ba ba boo*)
- What role do the backing singers have in the chorus? (*Add harmonies to the soloist*)
- In the first half of the chorus, does the bass play stepwise (scalic) notes, or jump around (arpeggios)? (*Stepwise*)

- In the middle 8 section, what instrument plays a solo? (*Percussion and drums*)
- Why does this song make you want to dance? (*Funky bass guitar and vocals, jazzy, exciting rhythmic parts*)

Activity 2: Stairway to Heaven (Led Zeppelin, 1971)

- What instrument begins the song? (*Acoustic guitar, finger-picking arpeggios*)
- Which woodwind instruments enter next? (*4 recorders*)
- When the faster section begins how does the guitar playing style change? (*Strumming chords*)

Activity 3: 'Autobahn' (Kraftwerk, 1974) – Minimoog centre stage

- What sound effects can you hear in the introduction? (*A lorry starting up, engine sounds*)
- Is the bassline is playing in intervals of octaves, thirds, or fifths? (*Octaves*)
- What kind of drum-kit is playing, acoustic or electronic? (*Electronic*)
- Is the vocal part a solo singer, or a voice doubled up? (*Doubled up*)

Activity 4: 'Anarchy in the UK' (Sex Pistols, 1976)

- How many chords do you hear in the introduction? (*4*)
- Describe the vocals. (*Out of tune, ugly sounding, spoken-style of singing, shouty, loosely sung*)
- Does the guitar sound clean or does it have a distortion effect? (*Distortion*)

Activity 5: 'Saturday Night Fever' (Bee Gees, 1977)

- What instruments feature in the introduction? (*Drums, bass guitar, synthesiser, strings*)
- Describe the pitch of the vocals. (*High*)
- In the chorus do the backing vocals sing in harmony and move together, or do they sing different parts? (in harmony and move together)

Activity 6: 'We Will Rock You' (Queen, 1977)
- What beats are the two stamps on? (*1 and 2*)
- What beat is the clap on? (*3*)
- What beat is the silence on? (*4*)
- How does the electric guitar enter? (*One-held note, growing in volume*)
- Does the electric guitar solo sound pre-composed or improvised? (*Improvised, although it is pre-composed*)

Activity 7: 'Who Are You?' (The Who, 1978)
- Describe the introduction. (*Cymbal clash and clap, repeated note sequence on synthesiser, improvised electric guitar solo; electric bass scalic part*)
- Describe the vocals in the introduction? (*High, long note, then short notes, choral sounding*)
- How does the chorus sound different to the verse?
  - o (*Chorus – choral vocals, octave electric bass, faster tempo, electric guitar imitates chorus vocals*)
  - o (*Verse – Rocky vocals, more drums in the fills, piano chords*)
- Are the bass guitar fills in the verses ascending or descending phrases? (*Descending*)

6.5.3 Playing
Activity 1: 'We Will Rock You' (Queen, 1977)
'We Will Rock You' (Queen, 1977) is an excellent song for children to practise basic beat skills, either using body percussion (clapping, stomping) or on untuned percussion or drums. Emphasise that there are 4 beats in a bar and get children to count with their voices if needed.

Activity 2: 'Rockin' All Over the World' (Status Quo, 1977)

Chord sequence	C, C, F, F
	C, G, C, G
Keyboards	chords of C (C, G, E)
Bass notes	C, E, G, A
Drum-kit	bass, snare and hi-hat

6.6 1980s

Rock music in the 1980s drew even bigger audiences with bands like Queen and events like Band Aid packing out huge stadiums. New wave music, influenced by the punk rock movement in the 70s, but more pop inspired, gained international recognition with artists including U2, Morrissey and Duran Duran. In 1981 MTV released their first-ever music video which was for the new wave band The Buggles with their song 'Video Killed the Radio Star' in 1981. Solo artists included Michael Jackson and Madonna who dominated the music charts globally. With developments in technology making instruments more accessible, the emergence of the synthesiser and drum machine in songs was a typical stylistic feature of many songs in the 80s.

6.6.1 Listening
Flash (Queen, 1980)
- How does the introduction create anticipation? (*Repeated bass note sounds like heartbeat*)
- Describe the vocals. (*Chorus singing together in harmony*)
- How many electric guitar parts can you hear play the fills? (2)
- What sound effects do you hear? (*Clips from the film* Flash Gordon, *laser beams*)
- How does the section change near the end? (*Piano accompaniment, solo singing, bassline*)

Activity 2: 'Thriller' (Michael Jackson, 1982)
The bassline is created from combining the sound of two modified Minimoogs.

- What sound effects can you hear at the start? (*Door creak, footsteps, wolf howling*)
- Is the sequence in the introduction ascending or descending in pitch? (*Ascending*)
- What instrument is playing the chords? (*Synthesiser*)

Activity 3: 'Master of Puppets' (Metallica, 1986)
- In the introduction does the riff ascend or descend? (*Descend*)
- Describe the tempo. (*Fast and energetic*)
- After the chorus, what word do the drums, vocals and guitar all play together? (*Master*)

Activity 4: 'Smooth Criminal' (Michael Jackson, 1987)
- Describe the introduction. (*Orchestral film music, similar to* E.T.)
- During the section of silence what sound effects can you hear? (*Door slam, finger bones crunch, whispering, cat purring, coin, jukebox turns on*)
- Describe the instrumentation? (*Synthesisers, drum machine, synth strings, bass guitar*)
- Is the drum beat played on the strong beat, or off-beat? (*Off-beat beats 2 and 4*)

Activity 1: 'It's A Sin' (Pet Shop Boys, 1987)
- What venue does the introduction sound like it should be played in? (*Church*)
- What instrument is playing the melodic parts? (*Synthesisers*)
- What weather sound effect can you hear? (*Thunderclaps*)
- Is the song in a major (happy) or minor (sad) key? (*Minor*)
- In the middle 8 section which begins, 'Father forgive me', how does the drum part change?
- How is the effect of monks chanting created?

Further listening suggestions
- 'Fools Gold' (The Stone Roses, 1989)
- 'Graceland' (Paul Simon, 1986)
- 'Jump' (Van Halen, 1984)
- 'Run to the Hills' (Iron Maiden, 1982)
- 'Going Underground' (The Jam, 1982)
- 'Should I Stay, or Should I Go' (The Clash, 1982)
- 'House of Fun' (Madness, 1982)
- 'Back in Black' (AC/DC, 1980)
- 'The Lovecats' (The Cure, 1983)

6.6.2 Singing

- 'Sweet Child of Mine' (Guns 'N Roses, 1987)
- 'Beat It', 'Smooth Criminal', 'Bad'(Michael Jackson)
- 'Vogue', 'True Blue' (Madonna)
- 'Take On Me' (A-Ha, 1985)
- 'Hounds of Love' (Kate Bush, 1985)
- 'Time After Time' (Cyndi Lauper, 1983)
- 'Total Eclipse of the Heart' (Bonnie Tyler, 1983)
- 'Eye of the Tiger' (Survivor, 1982)
- 'Tainted Love' (Soft Cell, 1981)

6.6.3 Playing

Activity 1: 'Another One Bites the Dust' (Queen, 1980)
This song works well with a basic 4 beat drum beat and can be played on keyboard and tuned percussion, although it sounds better on a guitar.

The notes of the bass riff are: E, E, E, E, E, G, E, A

Activity 2: 'Every Breath You Take' (The Police, 1983)
The chord sequence for this song is easy to play and the song has a steady enough tempo for classes to learn.

> Verse: G, Em, C, D, Em
> Chorus: C, G, A7, D

Activity 3: 'Livin' On a Prayer' (Jon Bon Jovi, 1986)
> Verse:
> Em, C, D
> Em, C, D, Em
> Bridge:
> C, D, Em x 4
> Chorus:
> Em, C, D, G, C, D
> Em, C, D, G, C, D Em

Activity 4: Bass riff from 'Thriller' (Michael Jackson, 1982)
Starting on beat 1: B, C#, E, F#, B

Activity 5: 'Axel F' – Theme from *Beverly Hill Cops* (Harold Faltermeyer, 1984)
The theme tune 'Axel F' from *Beverly Hill Cops* had a return when made popular (especially by young people) by Crazy Frog. Therefore, it works well as a keyboard riff to learn in the classroom:

Bass riff:

F, Ab, F, F, Bb, F, Eb
F, C, F, F, Db, C, Ab
F, C, F (8ve), F, Eb, Eb, C, G, F

6.7 1990s

The 1990s saw the emergence of boy-bands such as Take That and New Kids on the Block, as well as girl-bands such as the Spice Girls. Britpop arrived on the scene with bands like Oasis and Blur, writing rock songs about everyday life events, which were sung in British accents in a speech-style of singing. Techno and electronica developed during this decade and hip-hop and rap gained wider audiences, with the decade ending with the release of Eminem's first studio album.

6.7.1 Listening
Activity 1: 'Pump Up the Jam' (Technotronic, 1990)
- Is it an acoustic drum kit, or electronic drum machine? (*Drum machine*)
- What type of keyboard instrument is playing? (*Synth*)
- Describe the layers of instrumentation for both the verse and chorus. (*Drum machine rhythmic patterns, synth string chords, synth bass riff*)

Activity 2: 'Smells Like Teen Spirit' (Nirvana, 1991)
- Describe the instrumentation
- Write down the structure
- Describe the vocals

Activity 3: 'Wonderwall' (Oasis, 1995)
- How is the acoustic guitar being played? Strumming chords, or finger-picking? (*Strumming chords*)
- How many times is the chord sequence played in the introduction? (*4*)
- Describe the style of singing? (*Male, relaxed, a mix between singing and talking*)
- What string instrument is prominent in the song? (*Cello*)
- What percussion instrument can be heard clearly in the chorus keeping time? (*Tambourine*)

Activity 4: 'Spice Up Your Life' (Spice Girls, 1997)
- What is catchy about the introduction? (*Singing lalala, no words*)
- What styles of music have been an influence? Listen to the middle 8 section. (*Latin American*)
- What are the words that are shouted repeatedly in the refrain? (*'Spice up your life'*)
- What vocal technique is used in the chorus? (*Duet call and response*)

6.7.2 Singing
Here is a list of artists from the 1990s followed by suggestions of particular songs: Kylie Minogue, Madonna, Oasis, Ocean Colour Scene, Blur, R.E.M., Alanis Morrissette

- 'I Want It That Way' (Backstreet Boys, 1999)
- 'Hit Me Baby One More Time' (Britney Spears, 1998)
- 'Killing Me Softly with His Song' (Fugees, 1997)
- 'My Heart Will Go On' (Celine Dion, 1997)
- 'Gansta's Paradise' (Coolio, 1995)
- 'Don't Speak' (No Doubt, 1995)
- 'Creep' (Radiohead, 1993)
- Oasis have written many singable songs including 'Wonderwall', 'Don't Look Back in Anger', 'Champagne Supernova' and 'Half the World Away'

6.7.3 Playing
Activity 1: 'Bittersweet Symphony' (The Verve, 1997)
This piece works brilliantly in the classroom because the whole song is based a repeated chord sequence of 4 chords:

E, Bm, D, A

Activity 2: Come As You Are (Nirvana, 1992) – bass riff
The bassline for 'Come As You Are' is an excellent starting point for any beginner guitarists.

Activity 3: 'Gangsta's Paradise' (Coolio, 1995)
'Gangsta's Paradise'. The accompaniment chords to this song work really well for class ensemble.

1	2	3	4	1	2	3	4	1	2	3	4	1	2	3	4
D	D	D	D	C#	C#	D	A	D	D	D	D	C#	C#	D	E F
Bb	Bb	Bb	Bb	A	A	F	F	Bb	Bb	Bb	Bb	A	A	F	G A
Bb		G		A		D	A	Bb		G		A		D	A

6.8 2000s

The style of garage music had become popular towards the end of the 90s and this style continued strong into the 21st century with artists like Craig David reaching audiences globally. Emo ('emotive') music saw a generation of young rock fans get in touch with their emotions and Emo became a genre of youth voice and protest. Solo singers, rock bands and pop bands continued to be successful, although more electronic music entered the charts.

6.8.1 Listening
Activity 1: 'The Real Slim Shady' clean version (Eminem, 2000)
- Describe the introduction (*Synth organ riff and a synth bass riff playing together in harmony*)
- How many times do the instruments play the riff in the intro? (4)
- When does the drum machine come in? (*Same time as the singer*)

Activity 2: 'Pump It' (Black Eyed Peas, 2005)

What instrument starts the piece? (*Electric guitar fast picking*)

- How do the backing singers support the solo singer in the verse?
- What brass instrument has a melody line in the chorus? (*Trumpet*)
- What does the rhythm part consist of? (*A bass note on beat 1 followed by hand claps*)

Activity 3: 'The Pretender' (Foo Fighters, 2007)

- What instrument plays in the introduction? (*Electric guitar*)
- What happens to the tempo when the drum starts? (*Faster*)
- How is the drum played at the beginning of the verse? (*Single snare strike on the beat*)
- What is the role of the second vocal part in the chorus? (*Double up the lead singer, but adding a harmony*)

Activity 4: 'Bad Romance' (Lady Gaga, 2009)

- What instrument plays the introduction? (*Organ*)
- When the voice enters what instrument plays the accompaniment? (*Synthesisers*)
- Is the verse in a major or minor key? (*Minor*)

6.8.2 Singing

There are so many songs to choose from so here is a small selection:
- 'Umbrella' (Rhianna, 2008)
- 'Single Ladies' (Beyoncé, 2008)
- 'Rule the World' (Take That, 2006)
- 'Back to Black' (Amy Winehouse, 2005)
- 'Super Massive Black Hole' (Muse, 2005)
- 'Mr Brightside' (The Killers, 2004)
- 'Independent Woman' (Destiny's Child, 2001)
- 'Cha Cha Slide' ((DJ Casper, 2000)

6.8.3 Playing
Activity 1

'Seven Nation Army' (The White Stripes) has become very popularised and the guitar riff is associated with many other events, such as chants in sporting matches and political rallies (Jeremy Corbyn chant in the 2019 UK General Election).

The main guitar riff uses the notes – E, E, G, E, D, C, B – and can be played on any tuned instrument. It works well with students because the other part is the drum part which simply plays on the beats. The riff rhythm goes against the beat – syncopation – and so the sound of the two parts combined is very effective. Add the singing part and then you have a song working well in three parts which is manageable by a wide range of abilities.

This song has such a recognisable bass riff that most children already have it in their heads:

E E G E D C B

Activity 2: 'Boulevard of Broken Dreams' (Greenday, 2004)
Chord sequence:

> Verse – Em, G, D, A
> Chorus – C, G, D, Em

6.9 2010s–PRESENT

The recent developments in music genres have mostly come from Grime and Drill music. This music has rapping spoken in a London accent and is again an important youth voice. Often rap artists' lyrics raise awareness of important social and political issues such as inequality and gang culture. Stormzy has brought this style to the mainstream audience and the genre has a huge following. K-Pop (Korean pop) is extremely popular and there are many K-Pop bands well-known among young people.

6.9.1 Listening
Activity 1: 'Gangnam Style' (PSY, 2012)
- How many times does the riff play in the introduction? (8)
- What language is this song in? (*Korean*)

- Are the vocals sung, or rapped? (*Rapped more in the verse, sung in the chorus*)
- Do you know any of the associated dance moves?

Activity 2: 'Uptown Funk' (Mark Ronson, 2014)
- Describe the introduction (*Low voices scat the riff singing 'doh', off-beat claps, funky electric guitar riff*)
- What instrument accompanies the vocals at the beginning of the verse? (*Drums*)
- When the vocals stop what instruments are new to the piece? (*Brass section, synthesiser*)

Activity 3: 'Grace' (Stormzy, 2017)
- What is the first instrument playing? (*Church organ*)
- Describe the lead vocals (*Low bass voice, rapper*)
- Do the finger clicks happen on beats 1 and 3, or 2 and 4?
- What kind of choir is singing? (*Gospel*)

Activity 4: Listen to the album *Psychodrama* by the artist Dave
The album won the Mercury Award 2019 and is a superb example of how to write gritty lyrics about contemporary issues.
Writing rap/grime lyrics: Get the students to create a brainstorm of local, national or global issues that concern for your students.

6.9.2 Singing
- 'Me!' (Taylor Swift, 2019)
- 'Senorita' (Camilla Cabello, 2019)
- 'Shotgun' (George Ezra, 2018)
- 'Shallow' (Lady Gaga and Bradley Cooper, 2018)
- 'Big for Your Boots' (Stormzy, 2017)
- *The Greatest Showman* Soundtrack (2017)
- 'Shout Out to My Ex' (Little Mix, 2017)
- 'Believer' (Imagine Dragons, 2017)
- 'Shape of You' (Ed Sheeran, 2017)
- 'Stressed Out' (21 Pilots, 2015)
- 'Stay With Me' (Sam Smith, 2014)
- 'Roar' (Katy Perry, 2013)
- 'All of Me' (John Legend, 2013)

- 'Happy' (Pharrell Williams, 2013)
- 'Royals' (Lorde, 2013)
- 'Someone Like You' (Adele, 2011)

6.9.3 Playing
Activity: 'Diamonds' (Rhianna, 2013)
This song repeats the same chord sequence throughout the song –
G, Bm, A, F#m

CHAPTER 7
Music and technology

7.1 A HISTORY OF MUSIC TECHNOLOGY

Research the technological revolutions across the 20th and 21st century to gain an understanding of how technology has enhanced music production over the years as well as contributed to society. The history of sound recording can be divided into 4 periods:

- 1877–1925 – the 'Acoustic' era
- 1925–45 – the 'Electrical' era
- 1945–75 – the 'Magnetic era
- 1975–present – the 'Digital' era

7.1.1 Research activity
Trace the development of the following pieces of music technology and create a chronological timeline (Give a list to students in non-chronological order). Students can create a PowerPoint with pictures of each of these items of music technology. If possible, they can separate the technology into the four distinguishable eras, shown above. Students can also find pieces of music to demonstrate some early recordings of this technology:

Thomas Edison's phonograph (1877)
Microphone (1877)
Headphones (1910)
Theremin (1920)
Magnetic tape (1927)
Hammond organ (1929)
LP (1931)
AEG Magnetophon tape recorder (1935)

The vocoder (1940)
Transistor radio (1954)
Amplifier (1962)
Cassette tape (1963)
Moog synthesiser (1964)
8-track tape (1965)
Mini-Moog (1968)
Turntables (1972)
Walkman (1980)
CD – compact disc (1982)
Sampler (1986)
World Wide Web (1989)
Pro Tools (1991)
MP3 (1995)
iPod (2001)
iPad (2010)

Technology for guitars
Investigate how electric guitarists manipulate their sound. What is a guitar pedal? What are the different types? How do they alter the sound?

- What is the function of a guitar pedal and pedal board?
- How do these guitar pedals – wah-wah, whammy, fuzz box, tremolo, delay, echo – affect the sound?
- Find video clips on YouTube to illustrate a guitar begin played with one or more of these pedals.
- What is flanging?
- What is the difference in roles between a rhythm, lead and bass guitar part?
- When was the first amplifier invented and who by?

Microphones and vocoders
The ability to project and manipulate the voice has undoubtedly influenced artists in the last century. The microphone was invented by Alexander Graham Bell in 1876 and the wireless microphone in 1957 by Raymond A. Litke. If it is possible to get access to a microphone (and a speaker to amplify) in the classroom it can really inspire some children to perform better. Young people like to

experiment with their voice using technology and enjoy increasing the volume of their voice using microphones. Vocoders can be fun, especially when effects can change the pitch of a voice to make it incredibly high, or low sounding.

Synthesisers
Research the development of the synthesiser and create a chronological timeline of the following keyboard instruments. Also try to find an example of a piece of music that uses each instrument:

Mellotron; Moog; Theremin; Ondes martenot; Hammond organ; Korg Nord; clavinova

7.2 THE ROCK BAND

Rock bands rely on technology to amplify their sound to audiences. As technology develops so too do the instruments for rock bands to use.

The typical instruments used in a rock band are:

Lead singer	The person at the front of the band singing into a microphone, which is then plugged into an amplifier or PA.
Acoustic guitar	6 strings (nylon or steel), no need to plug in because the hollow body of the guitar serves as its own amplifier. Often brown in colour.
Electric guitar (lead/ rhythm)	6 strings, needs to be played by plugging a lead into an amplifier (large black box that looks like a speaker), often brightly coloured, and much thinner than an acoustic because it does not need a hollow body. Can also use effects pedals to alter the sounds of the guitar.
Bass guitar	4 strings, has a much longer neck than the other guitars, is much lower in sound, typically plays a bass riff or walking bass.
Drum-kit	The drum-kit typically consists of a bass/kick drum, floor tom, toms, snare, hi-hat, cymbals. The drummer uses drum-sticks to play the higher drums, and his feet to push the bass drum pedal. Some drummers choose to add many more drum components to give their rhythm a bigger sound.

7.2.1 Research activities
Activity 1
Draw or print-out a picture of a drum kit and label the following parts: kick/bass drum; snare drum; hi-hat; high tom; floor tom; low-hat; cymbals; hi-hat; ride cymbal.

What is (a) a rim shot; (b) a paradiddle; (c) a roll; (d) a backbeat?

Activity 2
Print out a picture of a guitar and label the following: tuning pegs; headstock; nut; frets; fingerboard; soundboard; soundhole; bridge; saddle; bridge pin; end pin; strap

Activity 3
Research the history of guitars and list the following in chronological order: Tanbur; Lute; Ud; 20th-century classical guitar; Vihuela; banjo, mandolin

7.2.2 Listening
Activity 1
Watch video clips of the students' favourite rock bands. Get them to describe what instruments are being used. Is the rock band using the typical rock band instrument set-up, or have they added more instruments, such as keyboards/synths, backing singers, or extra percussion?

Activity 2: Timelines and rock bands
Put the following rock bands in chronological order and research a song performed by each of them:

Queen, My Chemical Romance, Slipknot, Elvis Presley, The Beatles, Nirvana, Greenday, Sex Pistols, Foo Fighters

Activity 3: Labelling rock bands
Print out a picture of a rock band performing on stage. Get children to label the different instruments. Ask the question, *'How does a rock band use technology to make their music?'*

7.2.3 Playing
Activity 1: Guitar riffs
Popular electric guitar riffs to learn:

- 'Seven Nation Army' (The White Stripes, 2003)
- 'Under the Bridge' (Red Hot Chili Peppers, 1991)
- 'Smoke on the Water' (Deep Purple, 1972)
- 'Daytripper' (The Beatles, 1965)

Activity 2: Whole class band
Split the class up into 4 groups and give them a part of the rock band – one group takes on the rhythm section, one group the bass riff, one group the chords and the final group vocals. Choose a song which uses simple chord sequences and riffs, for example, 'Seven Nation Army' by The White Stripes. You can add other parts such as brass, backing vocals, and strings depending on the instrumentation of the song.

7.2.4 Composition
Activity
Most rock songs are based on a simple 4 chord sequence, or an interesting riff. Therefore to effectively compose a rock song it is a good idea to try to have both of these elements. It is preference as to whether the chords should be decided first, or the riff, but both must blend musically together, using similar harmonies.

7.3 EXPERIMENTAL MUSIC

Over the last 100 years music has embraced new technologies and freedoms which have enabled a more experimental approach to composition and performance. This progressive experimentation of sound began in the classical domain, with artists such as Cage and Stockhausen, and influenced popular musicians from the 1960s onward who mirrored the experimentation of sound in their genre of music. This resulted in music compositions which pushed boundaries in all the elements of music. Instrumentation included typewriters, kitchen utensils, helicopters, and aeroplane propellers. Harmonies moved towards more dissonant and clashing sounds, embracing the avant-garde approach of not giving harmonies resolutions. This chapter is split into rock and classical approaches to music experimentation.

7.4 PROGRESSIVE ROCK

Progressive rock is a movement of rock musicians who began to push the boundaries and experiment with aspects of music. Artists wanted to move beyond the 3 min single and therefore created longer tracks and embraced the 'concept' album, where all the tracks continue a common theme and act as one whole, rather than lots of independent tracks. Examples of prog rock bands are:

- King Crimson
- Pink Floyd
- Van Der Graaf Generator
- Genesis
- Yes
- Camel
- Proculharem
- Emerson, Lake and Palmer
- Frank Zappa

7.4.1 Listening activities
Activity 1: 'Interstellar', from *Piper at the Gates of Dawn* (Pink Floyd, 1964)
- Describe the guitar introduction (*Doubled up, 2 guitars playing, one moves up the octave after a while, descending scale*)
- How many times does the riff play in the introduction? (*4*)
- Does this music sound organised and predictable, or improvised and unpredictable? (*Improvised and unpredictable*)
- What makes this song experimental in style? (*Lots of effects on the guitars, little sense of pulse, irregular bar lengths, music being played over the bar-lines, some instruments in the foreground, others in the distance, lack of melody, atonal – no sense of key, lack of clear structure, unusual instrumentation, does not sound like a rock song, more like an art song*)

Activity 2: 'Revolution No. 9', from *The White Album* (The Beatles, 1968)
- Describe as many sounds as you can hear?
- Why is this piece experimental? (*It is made from a collage of random sound samples. It sounds chaotic, dissonant, atonal, clashing, fragmented and non-structured. It breaks traditional music composition rules of organising sound and pushes music boundaries*)
- What mood does it set? (*Not easy to listen to, uncomfortable*)

Activity 3: 'Hoe-down', from the ballet *Rodeo* (Aaron Copland, 1942)
(Also listen to *Billy the Kid* and *Appalachian Mountains* by Copland.)

Compare and contrast Copland's composition of a hoe-down with the arrangement by the progressive rock band Emerson, Lake and Palmer (ELP). Listen and list the similarities and differences between the two recordings:

Aaron Copland – 1942	Emerson, Lake and Palmer – 1972
Starts with cymbal clash	Drums
Full orchestra including harp, celeste and slap/whip stick.	Hammond organ
	Electronic synthesisers – moogs
Upbeat tempo	Gliss
No improvisation	Electronic guitar
	Effects used on the recording
	Similar upbeat tempo
	Section of improvisation

7.5 EXPERIMENTAL CLASSICAL MUSIC

7.5.1 Listening activities
Activity 1: *Helicopter String Quartet* (Karlheinz Stockhausen, 1995)
Watch one of the videos on YouTube of the performance to see the rare performance of 4 helicopters, each with a member of a string quartet. Discuss the piece with your class and ask the following questions:

- Can you describe how the instruments are being played? (*Scrubbing the strings – tremelando, glissando – sliding up and down the strings*)
- Do the instruments play together or do they sound like they are opposing each other? (*Opposing each other, clashing notes*)
- Why does this piece sound experimental? (*Atonal, no clear melody, untypical methods of playing string instruments, no clear structure or cohesion*)

Activity 2: Cage, John (1951) *Music for Changes* (composed using I Ching)
- What instrument is this piece for? (*Piano*)
- Does it sound random, or composed? (*Random*)
- Does the piece have a clear melody? (*No*)
- Is the playing scalic or angular? (*Angular*)
- Is the piece in a key, or atonal? (*Not in a key – no tonal centre, dissonant, atonal*)

Further listening: Experimental classical composers
Messiaen; Boulez; Xenakis; Berio; Schoenberg; Berg; Takemitsu

7.5.2 Composition
Chance music, or Aleatoric music as it is also known, can provide a wealth of composition ideas:

Activity: Composing music using a dice
Assign different elements of music to a dice and use it to make decisions on a piece of music. Using a dice substitute the numbers of the dice for 6 chords, for example, C, Dm, F, Am Bb, leaving one number for silence. Roll the dice and let chance decide on the sequence of chords.

Activity: Composing music using a pack of playing cards
Use a pack of cards and substitute individual cards for each of the 12 notes. Do the same for different note lengths. Play a card game and use the order of note names and lengths to compose a piece of music.

7.6 MINIMALISM

Minimalism is a style of experimental 20th century classical music based on short musical ideas that loop (repeat). Popular minimalist composers are Steve Reich, John Adams, Philip Glass, La Monte Young, Michael Nyman and Terry Riley. Minimalism began in the 1960s and influenced many other genres of music, for example club dance music and computer game music. Minimalist music is based on the repetition of a simple musical idea, which is repeated and then phased over the beats to create a different sense of pulse. Composers then alter the musical idea throughout the piece to give it more interest.

7.6.1 Listening activities
Activity 1: 'Facades' (Philip Glass, 1982)
- Can you hear a melody or lots of short musical ideas? (*Lots of short musical ideas*)
- Is there any repetition? (*Lots*)
- Describe the mood that this piece creates (*Ominous, something is happening, but not something good*)

Activity 2: 'Short Ride in a Fast Machine' (John Adams, 1986) – BBC Ten Pieces
- What instrument plays the constant beat throughout the piece? (*Woodblock*)
- Describe how the instruments are being played to give a sense of speed (*Fast short notes*)
- How does the music build in intensity? (*More instruments add to the texture, louder dynamics*)

Activity 3: 'Sextet for percussion and keyboards' (Steve Reich, 1984)
YouTube – Sextet, by Steve Reich (Full Performance) by Yale percussion group posted by Vic Firth [6 Apr. 2015] https://youtu.be/YgX85tZf1ts

7.6.2 Singing
A capella singing group Pentatonix is a great example of how to use the voice effectively to create repetitive patterns, as the musicians

use their voices to recreate the instrumental parts of songs, as well as the lead vocal parts. Pupils could create some short musical ideas and then build a vocal piece, or alternatively try to arrange a piece of minimalist music for a capella voices.

7.6.3 Playing
Activity 2: 'Clapping Music' (Steve Reich, 1972)
This is a popular, effective yet simple clapping piece of music that can help students develop rhythmic skills. It is based on 2 simple clapping parts, which overlap and therefore sound more interesting when played together.

In addition to this, there is a music app based around the piece which offers the player the same experience as you have to tap the screen in time to the beat given on the iPad while reading the notation.

Activity 3: 'Koyaaniqatsi' (Philip Glass, 1982)

Beats	1 2 3 4	1 2 3 4	1 2 3 4	1 2 3 4
Organ	- D F G A G F E	E C E F A G F E	E D F G A G F G	A Bb A Bb A G F E
Organ	D A D A D A D A	E A D A E A D A	D G D G D G D G	D A E A F A E A
Male voice	D D-- D D D---	D D-- D D D---	D D-- D D D---	D D-- D D D---
Bassline	D	C	Bb	F E D A

7.6.4 Improvising
Activity 1
One player starts playing a slow beat, the next player adds a beat, and so on, until the piece involves everyone and has built up. Naturally pupils will try to play on the same beat or fall into the sense of pulse. This time repeat the activity but ask players to avoid playing on the beat and to try to cause disruption. Players can count a cycle of beats in their head to keep in time with themselves.

Activity 2

Use the multitrack vocal recorder app *Loopy* to layer different musical ideas created by 6 people's voices. Each time the loop goes around, another person has to add another layer of sounds.

7.6.5 Composition
Activity 1

The first step in composing minimalist music is to come up with a short and simple musical idea. Set students a task of creating a short musical idea that will be easy to repeat. Once the musical idea has been created, then play around with that idea: play it back to front; upside down; augmented; diminished; using different harmonies.

Activity 2

Add rhythms to the following given notes to create short musical ideas. Choose one idea to base the composition around:

C, G, F, F, C
A, B, E, G, D, E
F, Ab, Bb, C
C, F, G
C, A, C, A, C, A, C, A
C, A, F, G

7.7 CLUB DANCE MUSIC

Dance music or Electronica is all based around using technology and computers to create music.

7.7.1 Listening activities
Activity 1: 'Sandstorm' (Darude, 1999)
- Describe the very first note of the piece (*Cymbal smash*)
- What happens to the drum beat when it enters (*Starts in the distance, gets louder, notes double*)

- Is the piece built using electronic or acoustic instruments? (*Electronic*)

Activity 2: 'Children' (Robert Miles, 1995)
- What instrument has the melodic part in the introduction? (*Piano*)
- What effect is added to this instrument? (*Echo*)
- What instrument adds the counter-melody? (*Acoustic guitar*)
- Describe the rhythm part and how it enters the song? (*Electronic drum machine, starts in the distance, gets louder, notes double*)

Further listening – electronic dance bands
- 'Right Here, Right Now'; 'Praise You'; 'Eat, Sleep Rave Repeat' (Fat Boy Slim)
- 'Born Slippy' (Underworld, 2000)
- 'Insomnia' (Faithless, 1995)
- Daft Punk
- Prodigy
- Pendulum
- Chase and Status
- Chemical Brothers
- Moby
- Skrillex

7.7.2 Playing
Activity 1: 'Children' (Robert Miles, 1995)
Piano notes:

1	2	3	4	1	2	3	4	1	2	3	4	1	2	3	4
F	F	F	F	F	F	Ab	G Eb	Eb	Eb	Eb	Eb	Eb	Eb	Ab	G C
1	2	3	4	1	2	3	4	1	2	3	4	1	2	3	4
C	C	C	C	C	C	Ab	G Ab	Ab	Ab	Ab	Ab	Ab	Ab	Ab	F G Ab C

Activity 2: 'No Limits' (2Unlimited, 1993)
Bass riff:

1	2	3	4	1	2	3	4	1	2	3	4	1	2	3	4
A	A	A	E A C	A	A	A	E A C	A	A	A	E A C	D	D	E	E

7.8 BEATBOXING

Beatboxing is a form of vocal percussion which first became recognised in the early 20th century. Over the last couple of decades, it has endured much more notoriety as a serious form of music-making. With the widespread reach and influence of the internet it is nowadays a very popular music skill for young people to practise.

7.8.1 Listening
Activity 1: Beardyman (Darren Foreman)– Beatbox demonstration
YouTube – Beardyman: 'Beatbox Recipe', posted by Outseeker [Nov 13, 2008] https://youtu.be/qd-8A6uQd6w

Activity 2: Riff Off – *Pitch Perfect 2* (rating 12):
Watch the riff off on YouTube and write down as many recognisable songs as possible in each of the categories.

- After the first category the treblemakers are asked to leave. What music style is chosen next for the beatboxing challenge? (*Country love*)
- Choose one of the songs and describe the other vocal layers singing over the beatbox beat.

7.9 DJING

The art of DJing – mixing/playing 2 or more music tracks together at the same time – is immensely popular across all generations. It is an easily accessible artform with many progression routes enabling the skill of using finely tuned aural skills to create accurate and exciting mixes.

There are many DJ style apps to download on mobile technology, meaning most young people have access to creating their own mixes, using their own portable music libraries. Using DJ hardware is more sensory and using DJ decks with portable LPs has a history of being a revered artform. DJs will always be required by the public for events such as parties and weddings.

7.9.1 Scratching

Every year the DMC World DJ Championships host a range of DJs competing for prizes and status. DJ Switch (Anthony Culverwell), representing the UK, won for three consecutive years starting in 2008 and many excellent clips can be seen on YouTube of how highly skilled this art form is. Be sure to check any YouTube clips of DJ mixing to ensure the clip is age appropriate.

7.9.2 Listening

Activity 1: 'Walk This Way' (Run DMC and Aerosmith, 1975)

- The song mixes a fusion of rock and hip-hop music. In what style does the song begin? (*Rock*)
- Describe the sound on the turntables during the first takeover section (*Scratching*)
- Describe the difference in vocal styles between the two bands.
  - (*Aerosmith – wide pitch range, screaming, forced powerful, singable*)
  - (*Run DMC – rapping, small pitch range, spoken lyrics, rhythm is important, reinforced words from other rappers*)

Activity 2: 'Concerto for Turntables and Orchestra' (Gabriel Prokofiev, 2009)

Watch the YouTube clip showing the 2011 Proms performance.

- How many times is the opening phrase repeated in the introduction? (*Twice*)
- What hand percussion instrument separates the introduction from the first section? (*Shakers*)
- What type of drums feature in the opening section? (*Drum kit*)

Further listening
- Grandmaster Flash
- DJ Jazzy Jeff

7.9.3 Composing
Activity
Listen to your own music and decide on two tracks you think would make a good DJ mix. Give reasons based on musical elements such as the tempo, keys and style.

Research task
How has dance music changed over the years? Think about the historical, geographical and social contexts. How has technology influenced this development? What is the difference between analogue and digital methods of DJing?

7.10 YOUTH CULTURE AND MUSICAL IDENTITY

Young people access music in a variety of ways. Access to more music than ever is now possible thanks to the developments of online platforms, YouTube and Spotify being notably popular. Smart phones have become part of young people's identity and since 2010 mobile technology in general has increased the amount and range of music that young people can listen to as well as allowing them greater technical scope and flexibility to make music at home as 'bedroom musicians'.

Activity 1: *X Factor*
Watch some of the *X Factor* auditions and take note of how the judges give feedback. Ask the students:

- What do they think of the audition and why?
- Do they think the judges give positive or negative feedback?

A creative idea is to make Simon Cowell masks so that the children can give each other feedback in the guise of Mr Cowell. This can lower the children's inhibitions and empower them to give more candid feedback, especially if they are nervous.

Activity 2: Karaoke

Whether pupils are singing an unrehearsed song on the spot, or a pre-rehearsed song, karaoke is a widely accepted and embraced form of musical performance. Children are so used to seeing people perform in this style on TV that many aspire to being able to sing using a microphone too. Karaoke cannot be underestimated as to the value it can have on inspiring young people to sing and perform. Access to a speaker and microphone is useful, and all schools should have a sharable resource such as this. YouTube contains lyric versions of nearly all popular songs, and karaoke versions (with no singing on the track) too.

Activity 3: Karaoke competition

Host a karaoke competition at the school. Get students to design posters, hold auditions, choose some judges and prizes. Students sing the first 1.30 minutes of their favourite song, hopefully from memory, and compete in giving the most memorable performance. Stylistic criteria for judges to mark against could be: lyrics memorised; intonation (tuning); accuracy (timing); musicality; expression; choice of song (suitability for male/female voice, too high/low).

Activity 4: Talent show

Many young people watch talent shows such as *Britain's Got Talent* and *Strictly Come Dancing*. The format of some of these shows provides inspiration for more classroom activities. Young people love the opportunity to share any talent they have, and talent shows are generally a real success when put on in schools. These can be musical, or general talent shows. Auditions can work well and give the students a real sense of competition, meaning they might perform even better, although some might become more nervous.

Activity 5: Music awards

Help pupils to research the most recent music awards – Brit Awards, MTV Awards, Mercury Awards, Mobo Awards. They must find out the following:

- Who is/was nominated for this year's award?
- Who is the favourite to win the award this year?
- What artists won the previous years' awards?
- What is the prize?
- Listen to some of the nomination's music on YouTube and write who your favourite nominee is/was and give reasons.

7.11 ACCESSING MUSIC AND ACCESSIBLE MUSIC-MAKING

7.11.1 Streaming
Find out which methods students use to access their music. Popular music streaming platforms are: Spotify; Amazon Music; Google Play; Apple Music

7.11.2 Social media
Social media apps offer platforms for people to share music: Instagram, Snapchat, Facebook, Twitter, Tiktok

7.11.3 Youtubers and subscriptions
Many young people subscribe to youtubers to follow their YouTube channel and keep up to date with the youtubers latest posts online. This is overtaking time spent watching TV and is a preferred past-time for relaxation. Especially because YouTube can be accessed online anywhere as long as there is WiFi. It is easy and popular for young people to become youtubers and create their own YouTube channel, enabling friends to subscribe to them and see any films they post. Being creative in this way is an excellent method for young people to socialise and develop skills such as film-making, presenting and creativity.

7.11.4 Podcasts
Podcasts are short programmes of recorded voice and are often documentary and informative in style, whether educational, interviews or storytelling.

7.11.5 Recommended computer music programmes
GarageBand; Logic Pro; Audacity; Soundtrap; Protools; Tidel Sank; Adobe Audition; Avid; Slate; BandLab; Cakewalk; Cubase.

Soundtrap is an online music making program used in both school and home settings. It offers samples and loops for people to create their own music and because of its easy accessibility and communicability is used in schools across the country.

7.11.6 Computer consoles and games
- PlayStation and Xbox – Rock Band, Guitar Hero, Rocksmith, Just Dance, Singstar
- Wii – music games – conduct an orchestra

7.12 INCLUSIVE TECHNOLOGY

7.12.1 Eye gazers and eye gazer technology:
Eye gazers and eye gazer technology have enabled instrumental learning and ensemble music-making to be more inclusive. They assist people who have difficulties accessing traditional instruments and computers, and involve the user, or musician, inputting data using the movement of their eye. Musicians using this technology can be seen performing with the British Paraorchestra and the National Open Youth Orchestra (NOYO).

7.12.2 Switch technology
Switch technology consists of large buttons, or switches, which can be connected through devices to help people who may have difficulties with their fine motor skills. This technology can help some young people join in with music-making by interacting and being proactive with sound.

7.12.3 Virtual reality concerts
Virtual reality is a great way of being fully immersive with music. Bjork worked with film directors to create a 360 degrees virtual world to accompany her 2014 album *Vulnicura*. VR concerts are happening more often; however, they cost more money for the artists to invest in.

7.12.4 Mi.Mu gloves
Watch the YouTube clip of Imogen Heap demonstrating Mi.Mu gloves at a Ted Talk. This really demonstrates the futuristic developments of creating accessible music technology.

YouTube – Sculpting music with Mi.Mu gloves / Imogen Heap / TEDxCERN [7 Dec. 2015] posted by TedxTalks

7.13 IPAD MUSIC

Mobile technologies can be used as instruments to play music. They can also be used as aids for improvisations, tools for composition and songwriting as well as listening devices. Currently app developers favour making apps for iPhones and iPads, so Apple holds the monopoly on music app developers and music apps.

The internet is a helpful source as there is an ever-increasing range of teacher suggested apps and tutorials on YouTube; however, this can be time-consuming. The more fun you have exploring apps, and the more musically creative you can be will help to deliver higher-quality music lessons. Watching YouTube clips of iPad bands is definitely a recommendation as these can be inspiring and demonstrate what to aim for when making music with iPads.

7.13.1 Apps to develop listening and aural skills
- My First Classical Music App
- The Orchestra
- Meet the Orchestra app
- The History of Jazz app
- Music for Little Mozart
- Young Person's Guide to the Orchestra app
- Ear Wizard

7.13.2 Apps to develop singing skills
- Smule Karaoke
- Smule Autorap
- Improvox
- Vio
- Starkaraoke
- Loopy
- Keezy

7.13.3 Apps to develop improvisation skills

- Airvox
- Music Sparkles
- Fingertip Maestro
- Iambeatbox
- Impaktor
- Geosynth
- Nodebeat
- Scape

7.13.4 Apps to develop playing skills

Chords:
- o Soundprism and Soundprism Electro

Developing sense of beat skills:
- o Magic Piano
- o Keezy Drummer
- o Monkey Drum
- o Epic Orchestra
- o iDaft
- o Steve Reich's Clapping Music
- o Kids tap-along
- o Bebot

Samples:
- o Rayman's Beatbox Legends
- o Dubpad
- o Launchpad

Instruments:
- o GoGoXylo
- o iFretless Brass/sax/guitar/bass
- o Rockmate
- o ThumbJam
- o Geosynth

7.13.5 Apps to develop composition skills

Multitrack recorders:
- o GarageBand
- o iMachine
- o Toc and Roll

CHAPTER 8
Music from around the globe

When teaching music around the globe it is important to learn about the music in a variety of contexts: historical, cultural, political and geographical. This makes global music adaptable to fit into other subject disciplines. This chapter contains ideas and activities about the music in different continents around the world, covering a range of music genre.

- Europe
- Africa and Arabia
- The Americas
- Asia and Oceania

8.1 EUROPE

8.1.1 Eurovision
The Eurovision song contest is a fun resource for looking at representatives of modern music across Europe. A compilation CD/recording is released each year and is a great discussion point for students to develop their critical engagement skills.

Alternatively get students to trace the development of popular music by listening to various entries from the UK, or other countries, through the years. What do they notice about how music has changed? Has technology played a role?

8.2 THE MEDITERRANEAN

The Mediterranean evokes images of sun, sea, and relaxation. Music contrasts between the traditional folk music from countries such as Greece, Italy and Croatia, with the island of Ibiza, famous for its DJs, clubs and dance music.

Spain has a long tradition of Flamenco music, with virtuosic Spanish guitar playing and dances of passion with castanets and stamping feet. Spanish composers include: Isaac Albéniz, Manuel De Falla and Joaquín Rodrigo. Portugal has a tradition of Fado songs dating back to the early 19th century.

8.2.1 Listening
Activity 1: Spain – 'Asturias (Leyenda)' (Isaac Albeniz, 1892)
- Is this piece in a major or minor key? (*Minor*)
- How is the classical guitar being played? (*Finger-picking*)
- How does the piece build up? (*Gets louder, more notes, strum chords on the string beats*)
- In the quiet middle section is the melody played in octaves (the same note) or in harmonies? (*In octaves*)

Activity 2: Greece – 'Zorba's Dance' (Mikis Theodorakis, 1964)
- What type of instrument is this piece being played on? (string – mandolin and bouzouki)
- On what beats does (a) the bass play, (b) chords? (*(a) 1 and 3; (b) 2 and 4)*
- What happens to the tempo throughout the piece? (*Speeds up*)

Activity 3: Ludovico Einaudi (1955–present)
Italian contemporary composer Ludovico Einaudi composes not only film scores, but reflective music about the world he encounters. Listen to pieces from his latest album – *Seven Days Walking* (2019) and discuss the mood and atmosphere created by some of the different pieces.

8.2.2 Singing
Popular music sung in either the Spanish or Portuguese language has had success with several songs over the years:

- 'Despacito' (Luis Fonsi, 2019)

- 'La Respuesta' (Becky G and Maluma, 2019)
- 'Asereje' (the Ketchup song) (Las Ketchup, 2002)
- 'Macarena' (Los Del Río, 1993)
- 'La Bamba' (Ritchie Valens, 1958)
- Lambada (Kaoma, 1989) – sung in Portuguese

8.3 FRENCH MUSIC

French music is typically known for cabaret songs, can-can music and chanson; impressionist composers such as Debussy and Ravel; French jazz and electronic music, with influential artists such as Jean Michel Jarre and Daft Punk. French hip-hop bands such as Saîan Supa Crew and artists such as Stromae and Indila, and globally recognised DJs such as Kungs.

8.3.1 Listening
Activity 1: 'Galop Infernal', from the operetta *Orpheus in the Underworld* (Jacques Offenbach, 1858)
- What type of ensemble is performing this piece? (*Orchestra*)
- The introduction is a musical conversation between which 2 instrumental families? (*Strings and woodwind*)
- What percussion instrument is prominent? (*Triangle*)
- Why does this music suit a can-can dance? (*High energy makes you want to dance*)

Activity 2: 'Non, Je ne regrette rien' (Edith Piaf, 1956)
- Is the singer male or female? (*Female*)
- What language are they singing in? (*French*)
- Does the accompaniment have straight or swung sounding rhythms? (*Swung*)
- How many bass notes can you hear? (4)
- When does the harp enter? (*Second verse*)

8.3.2 Singing
'Frère Jacques' is a French nursery rhyme translated meaning Brother John. It can be sung in a musical round and there are lots of recordings on YouTube to help with this.

Frère Jacques, x2
Dormez-vous? x2
Sonnez les matines! x2
Ding, dang, dong. x2

'Alouette' is a traditional French-Canadian folk song about a lark. It works well with young children and is a good introduction into singing in a different language.

Chorus:
Alouette, gentille aloutte,
Alouette, je te plumerai.
Verse 1:
Je te plumerei la tête. X2
Et la tête! X2
Alouette! X2
A-a-a-ah

8.4 GERMANY, AUSTRIA AND SWITZERLAND

The Alps mountain range conjures up an image of Alpine horns and yodelling, while the style of waltzes and polkas traditionally come from German dance music.

8.4.1 Listening
Activity 1: 'The Blue Danube', Op. 314 (Johann II Strauss, 1825–99)
- What type of ensemble plays this piece? (*Orchestra*)
- What instruments play first? (*French horns*)
- During the introduction how are the strings played in the accompaniment? (*Tremolando, scrubbing the bow on the string, shimmering*)
- How many beats are there in a bar? (*3*)
- Does the tempo remain the same speed? (*No, it keeps changing until the main waltz starts*)
- Do the beats sound perfectly on the beat, or slightly off? (*Slightly off*)

Activity 2: 'The Lonely Goatherd', from *The Sound of Music* **(Rodgers and Hammerstein, 1965)**
- Is the singer male or female? (*Female*)
- Do the children singing the chorus sing words, or yodel? (*Yodel*)
- What brass instrument plays the melody in the second chorus? (*Tuba*)

8.5 EASTERN EUROPE

Many Eastern European countries are influenced by music from around the world and have strong traditions in genre such as jazz (musicians like Tomasz Stan/ko) and death metal (bands include Behemoth and Vader).

8.5.1 Listening
Classical composers in Eastern European countries have collected traditional folk songs and arranged them into new music. Here is a list of composers to listen to:

Poland	Penderecki (1933–present), Górecki (1933–2010)
Hungary	Bartok (1881–1945)
Russia	Mussorgsky (1839–81) Rimsky-Korsakov (1844–1908) Shostakovich (1906–75) Tchaikovsky (1840–93)
Estonia	Arvo Pärt (born 1935)

8.6 NORDIC COUNTRIES

8.6.1 Listening
- Bjork
- Sigur Rós
- Of Monsters and Men
- Skálmöld
- *Frozen* and *Frozen 2* (2013 and 2019) soundtracks
- *Finlandia* (Jean Sibelius, 1865–1957)
- Abba

- Yngwie Malmsteen
- Carl Nielsen (1865–1931)

8.6.2 Composing
Activity 1: Songwriting – myths and legends
Icelandic folk songs dating back to the 14th century have revealed many themes including trolls, elves and other mythical creatures, and legends. Use a Nordic folk story to inspire a musical composition.

Activity 2: Aurora borealis
The aurora borealis is a spectacular sight, especially over the stark icy landscapes of parts of the Northern hemisphere. Use photos, or a YouTube clip to compose tranquil, meditative types of music. Use the techniques of minimalism, repetition of short music ideas, modal harmonies and drones.

8.7 AFRICAN MUSIC

Many countries in Africa have their own cultural musical styles. African drumming (djembe and talking drums) is very popular, therefore rhythm plays a strong role in African music. Singing is also very popular, and the continent is rich with singing being embedded into many parts of African life. Traditional African folksongs are passed orally and are often sung using call and response and multi-layered harmonies. The modern style of Afrobeat, and the influence of African music in fusion styles influences many artists from around the globe.

8.7.1 Listening activities
Activity 1: 'Inkanyezi Nezazi' (Ladysmith Black Mambazo, 1999)
- Are the voices male, female, or both? (*Male*)
- Does the choir sing in homophony (all parts moving together) *or* polyphony (all parts moving at different times)? (*Homophony*)

- Does the choir sing the same note or sing in harmonies? (*Harmonies*)
- Other than singing what sounds do they use in the piece? (*Gulping, clicking*)

Activity 2: Ali Farka Touré and Toumani Diabaté – Debe live at Bozar [19 May 2011] World Circuit Records: https://youtu.be/pJUE03aeaQ4

- The African string instrument is called a kora; how is it played? (*Plucking with thumbs and fingers, similar to a harp*)
- What role does the acoustic guitar play? (*Repeating phrase, accompaniment, riff/ostinato*)
- Is the piece in a major or minor key? (*Major*)
- Describe the mood of the piece (*Peaceful, quiet, calm, cheerful, soft*)

Further listening

African instruments:

kora, sansa (thumb piano), mbira, balafon, djembe, talking drum

African/Afrobeat artists:

Fela Kuti, Femi Kuti, Tony Allen, Oumou Sangare, Cheikh Lo, Angelique Kidjo, Baaba Maal, Sierra Leone Refugee Allstars

Fusion:

'Under African Skies' and 'Homeless' from the album *Graceland* (Paul Simon, 1986)

African Sanctus (David Fanshawe, 1969)

Film:

The Lion King, Madagascar, Born Free

8.7.2 Singing

Activity 1: 'The Lion Sleeps Tonight' ('Wimoweh') (The Tokens, 1961)

This song has been recorded by many artists. A really child-friendly version can be seen on YouTube by Hippo Pat and Dog Stanley [23 Aug. 2013] posted by Brimenting: https://youtu.be/oNcAs1iW-Us

Activity 2: 'Che Che Koolay' – traditional song from Ghana

Call:	Response:
Che che koolay	Che che koolay
Che che kofeesa	Che che kofeesa
Kofee salanga	Kofee salanga
Kaka shee langa	Kaka shee langa
Whoops ah lay lay	Whoops ah lay lay

8.7.3 Playing
Activity: Djembe drumming

African djembe drums can be played by slapping/hitting/striking different areas of the drum in different ways. To get the bass sound, strike the centre of the drum, lifting your hand once you have played the note. This sound is called 'Dun' if played on the left and 'Gun' on the right. Slapping the drum on the front edge of the djembe is called Ta (left) and Pa (right), while the more tonal sounds are played in-between the edge and the centre, 'Do' on the left and 'Go' on the right.

Left	Ta		Ta	Ta		Ta		
Right		Pa			Pa		Pa	Pa

8.7.4 Improvisation

Use phrases to create some basic djembe rhythms and play in a call and response style to a basic beat of 4:

Leader:	Response:
Can you play djembe?	I can play djembe
Can you play djembe?	I can play djembe
Do you want to play?	Yes, we want to play?
OK	OK

8.7.5 Composition
Activity: Rhythm grids

Here is an example of a cyclic rhythm grid. The idea is to count the beats out loud 2 or 3 times in a row, and clap on the beats which are marked with an X.

1	2	3	4	5	6	7	8	9	10	11	12
X			X		X	X			X	X	
	X			X			X			X	X
X		X			X	X		X			

Students can have blank rhythm grids and choose their own beats.

Instead of clapping, add djembe or other instruments.

8.8 ARABIAN MUSIC

Arabian music sounds exotic and immediately conjures up images of the desert, mirages of oasis, camels and bedouins. This is mainly because of the Arabic scale and the melodic modes – maqam – of which there are 40. These can be heard in 22 Arab states, including countries such as Egypt and Morocco. Arabic music uses a particular rhythm – Rajaz – which sounds like camel hooves in the sand. It can sound like this: Tea – & Cof-fee

8.8.1 Listening activities
Activity 1: YouTube – Musicians of the Nile – 'Tayyara' (medium arghul) [27 Apr. 2013] posted by Angel Tonchev: https://youtu.be/_AnXCubuAzc

Listen to a recording of 'Tayyara' by Musicians of the Nile (on YouTube):

- The first note acts as a drone to the melodic line that sounds improvised over the top. Does the drone change note at all? (*No*)
- Describe the sound of the arghul (*Nasal, reed-like, like an oboe, harsh*)

- What function do the drums provide? (*They add the beat and rhythms*)
- What happens to the tempo throughout the song? (*Speeds up*)
- What term do we give the technique of over-blowing a note to change its pitch? (*Pitch-bending*)

The arghul is a traditional Arabic musical instrument which has been used since ancient times. It has two pipes – one to play the drone (held note) and the other to play a melody (five – seven holes). The instrument has a single reed and sounds slightly similar to a clarinet. There are 3 types of arghuls: small, medium and large. It is used to accompany belly dancing.

Activity 2: *Lawrence of Arabia* **Theme (Maurice Jarre, 1962)**
The introduction section is loud and full of energy:

- What happens at the change of section, when the main theme starts? (*Quieter, slower*)
- What instrument plays the main theme initially? (*Flute*)
- What instruments join in for the section playing? (*Strings*)
- Is the accompaniment based on scales or arpeggios? (*Arpeggios*)

Activity 3: Tutankhamun's trumpets
Two trumpets – one bronze, one silver – were discovered under Tutankhamun's burial chamber in 1922 by Howard Carter. They are the oldest known surviving working trumpets. Listen to the sound on the BBC recording from 1939 (YouTube)

King Tutankhamun's Trumpets Played After 3000+ Years [1 June 2014] posted by Joe Kiernan: https://youtu.be/Qt9AyV3hnlc

- Compare the sound of the old trumpets to a modern day one. What are valves? When were valves invented? How does a trumpet sound different with valves?

8.8.2 Singing
Arabian songs for young people are tricky to find because of the language. Therefore, songs about Arabian culture may work better. Here are a couple of suggestions for singing or further listening:

- 'Alice the Camel' – traditional children's song
- 'Walk Like an Egyptian' (The Bangles, 1986)
- 'A Whole New World', from Disney's *Aladdin* (Alan Menken, 1992)
- Moroccan pop – Oussama Belhcen (born 1991)
- Hossam Ramzy (1953–2019)

8.8.3 Improvisation

Similar to other styles of world music, Arabian music has a two-note drone, which is then improvised over with a scale of notes. The Arabic scale typically has the following notes: C, Db, E, F, G, Ab, Bb, C. Students can improvise over a drone using the notes C and G. If there are too many notes to begin with, break down the scale into smaller steps.

In Arabic music some chords are given names to represent a specific combination of notes. The Nikriz pentachord, starting on C, is a good selection of notes to capture an exotic flavour for an improvisation – C, D, Eb, F#, G.

8.8.4 Composition

Activity 1

Use the story of Lawrence of Arabia to create a song. Write lyrics depicting the story and using the Rajaz rhythm and Arabic scale compose an accompaniment to the song. Use a combination of Western and Eastern influences, for example add drums or finger cymbals.

Activity 2

Compose an atmospheric piece to depict the mood of the desert, a journey on a camel, or trip along the Nile river. Write a description of the story and make decisions how to create music for each section.

Activity 3

Compose an upbeat song to sell goods at an Arabian market. Write lyrics to describe what you might sell in a bazaar – spices, rugs, olives.

8.9 UNITED STATES OF AMERICA

Music from the USA covers a range of styles from different states across the north, south, east and west coasts, and from different periods of history. Country music remains very popular across the states and there is a huge country music scene. Artists past and present include Dolly Parton, Garth Brooks, Tammy Wynette and Johnny Cash. Blues music has influenced many jazz and popular styles of music, while many other music styles include: Cajun and Creole music; Appalachian music; Native American music; Bluegrass; and Hawaiian music.

8.9.1 Listening
Activity 1: 'The Star-Spangled Banner' (American national anthem) (John Stafford Smith, c. 1773)
- What type of drum introduces the song? (*Snare/side drum*) What technique is used to play it? (*Drum roll*)
- What family of instruments play first? (*Brass*)
- Are the rhythms played straight or swung? (*Swung*)

Activity 2: 'Working 9 to 5' (Dolly Parton, 1980)
- What instrument plays in the introduction and first verse? (*Piano*)
- How are the chords being played in the verse? (*Repeated held chords*)
- What device is the percussion trying to emulate in the verse? (*Typewriter*)
- What brass instruments can you hear in the chorus? (*Trumpet, trombone, saxophone – although this is a wind instrument*)

Activity 3: 'The Thunder Rolls' (Garth Brooks, 1998)
- What weather sound effect is added over the song? (*Thunder rolls*)
- What instrument is accompanying the singer? (*Acoustic guitar*)
- What instruments join in during verse two? (*Drum kit, bass guitar, lead guitar*)
- Is the song in a major or minor key? (*Minor*)

Activity 4: 'Rhapsody in Blue' (George Gershwin, 1924)
- What wind instrument features prominently in the piece? (*Clarinet*)

- What technique is used to play the introduction, moving from the low notes up to the high notes? (*Slide/glissando*)
- Is the tempo strict or relaxed in the introduction? (*Relaxed*)
- What instrument features that is not normally typical in an orchestra? (*Piano*)

8.9.2 Singing
North-American folk songs

- 'She'll Be Coming 'Round the Mountain' (trad. American folk song)
- 'On Top of Old Smoky' (trad. American folk song, origins unknown)
- 'The Yellow Rose of Texas' (trad. American folk song, c. 1850s)
- 'Home on the Range' (Daniel E. Kelly, c. 19th century)
- 'Streets of Laredo' ('Cowboy's Lament') (Frank H. Maynard, c. 1910)
- 'Old Town Road' (Lil Nas featuring Billy Ray Cyrus, 2019)

8.9.3 Dancing
Activity: Line-dancing – developing a sense of beat and rhythm
Line-dancing is where people dance a sequence of steps in rows/ lines, facing different directions as the song progresses. Learn a line-dance using a YouTube tutorial. Get students to choreograph their own line-dance routine. They could do this in teams and teach the rest of the class. The band The Woolpackers have released a variety of appropriate songs to line dance to.

8.10 LATIN AMERICAN MUSIC

Music is the heart and soul of Latin American countries, which are rich with musical flavour and interest. There are many styles of music across Latin America, from reggae in Jamaica, rumba from Cuba, and samba from Brazil. Recognisable styles of Caribbean music include dancehall, reggae, reggaetón, salsa, calypso songs and steel pan music. Music is structured around rhythms that are handed down by generations and many songs are passed through the oral tradition. Key features of Latin American music are: rhythm, percussion, Spanish/Portuguese lyrics, carnivals, brass sections and dancing.

8.10.1 Listening
Activity 1: Havana (Camila Cabello, 2019)
What instrument plays in the introduction? (*Piano*)
Describe the rhythm part (*Offbeat claps, then added percussion, cowbell*)
What type of bass plays? (*Bass guitar*)
What role do the backing singers have in the verse? (*Fills, then they add harmonies to the lead singer*)

Activity 2: I Like It Like That (Pete Rodriguez, 1967)
What instrument plays in the introduction? (*Piano*)
Describe the rhythm part (*Offbeat claps, then added percussion, cowbell*)
What type of bass plays? (*Double bass*)
What brass instrument joins in? (*Trumpet*)

Activity 3: Harry Belafonte sings a calypso song with The Muppets
Watch the clip of Harry Belafonte singing with The Muppets. YouTube – Muppet Songs: Harry Belafonte – 'Day-O' ('Banana Boat Song') posted by Muppet Songs [11 Sep. 2018] https://youtu.be/P-4xyg4PU-U

- Does the introduction have an accompaniment? (*No, it is sung a capella*)
- Describe the accompaniment during the song (*Bass guitar and bongo drums*)
- What role do the backing singers have? (*They sing in harmony, responding to the call*)
- What is the deadly creature in the song lyrics? (*Tarantula*)

8.10.2 Further listening, and singing
- 'Despacito' (Luis Fonsi, Daddy Yankee and Justin Bieber, 2019)
- 'Chantaje' (Shakira ft. Maluma, 2016)
- Buena Vista Social Club (1996–present)
- 'Mambo No. 5' (Lou Bega, 1999)
- Jamaican Farewell' (Harry Belafonte, 1957)
- 'Oye Como Va' (Tito Puente, 1956)
- 'Day-O' ('Banana Boat Song') (traditional, c. late-19th century)

8.10.3 Playing
Lots of typical classroom percussion can include instruments from Latin-America, including bongos, guiro, claves, cabassa, maracas, and agogo bells. Samba kits are mostly affordable for schools and pupils can learn about the different types of percussion and rotate the different percussion roles when playing.

Activity 1: Musical canon
'Anytime You Need a Calypso' (Jan Holdstock) – sing this song in a musical round. Once mastered add the accompanying chords.

Chords:
    D, G, A7, D

Activity 2: 'Jamaican Farewell' (Harry Belafonte, 1957)
Chord sequence:
    Verse
        G, C, G, G
        G, C, D, G
    Chorus
        G, C, D, G
        G, C, D, G

8.10.4 Composing
Activity: Samba percussion
Explore the following Brazilian percussion instruments and compose some rhythmic pieces based on basic Latin rhythmic ideas:

Claves, guiro, maracas, cowbell, vibra-slap, bongos, congas, timbales, ago-go, claves, triangle, woodblock, surdo drums, tamborim, cabasa, reco-reco, pandeiro.

The band leader must work out a call on a samba whistle and lead the group once the rhythms have been decided.

Here is the basic 3/2 rhythm:

Beat	1	+	2	+	3	+	4	+
Clave		X	X		X	X		X

8.10.5 Dancing
Activity 1: Limbo dancing
This is the unofficial national dance for the islands of Trinidad and Tobago. It involves people taking turns to dance underneath a pole, with their backs to the floor, in a bid not to have any body part touch the pole and therefore be out of the competition. After each round the pole is lowered and the winner is the last dancer. It is a great icebreaker activity and is still used as a welcome game for tourists when they visit the Caribbean. Songs which have popularised the limbo are Chubby Checker's 'Limbo Rock' (1987) and Brigo's (Samuel Adams) 'Limbo Break' (1998).

8.10.6 Research
Activity: Carnival
Put on a carnival at your school and research music from South America to create a soundtrack. Research the following styles of music:

- Bossa nova
- Cha-cha-cha
- Mambo
- Bolero
- Rumba
- Argentine tango
- Salsa

8.11 JAMAICAN MUSIC – REGGAE

The roots of reggae music lie in the cultural identity of the music and musicians playing music in the 1940s on the Caribbean island of Jamaica. Sound-systems were cheaper than live musicians, therefore music was shared more commercially, and many Jamaicans listened to American R&B (rhythm and blues) music on the radio.

The musical characteristics of reggae music which give it a unique feel are:

- A strong bass-riff.
- Often the song has simple chord sequences of 2 or 3 chords.
- The chords are played on the 2nd and 4th beat of a 4/4 bar, giving the music a strong offbeat and lilting feel.
- Often has political or religious lyrics associated with Jamaica or Rastafarianism.

8.11.1 Listening
Activity 1: 'No Woman, No Cry' (Bob Marley and the Wailers, 1975)
- What type of keyboard instrument is playing? (*Hammond organ*)
- What effect is used on the guitar? (*Wah-wah pedal*)
- Is the bassline scalic or angular (jumpy)? (*Scalic*)
- Are Bob Marley's vocals strict or relaxed? (*Relaxed*)
- What beats are emphasised by the percussion? (*Offbeat – 2 and 4*)

Activity 2: 'Make It Bun Dem' (Skrillex and Damian 'Jr. Gong' Marley, 2012)
- What beats are the chords played on? (*Offbeat – 2 and 4*)
- Do the vocals sound strict or relaxed over the beat? (*Improvised*)
- What style of electronic music has been influenced by reggae and typically can be recognised by large wobble synth sounds? (*Dubstep*)

8.11.2 Playing
Activity: 'Three Little Birds' (Bob Marley, 1977)
    Chord sequence:
    A (E C# E), A, D (A F# A), A

A (E C# E), A, D (A F# A), A
A, E (B G# B), A, D
A, E, D, A

8.11.3 Research
Activity: Caribbean music
Produce a research page on one of the following aspects of Caribbean music:

- Create a poster for a reggae concert giving facts about the style of reggae and listing 3 famous reggae artists.
- On a blank map of the Caribbean label as many islands as you can find out.
- Choose a Caribbean flag to paint and colour it in with the correct colours.
- Create a PowerPoint about Bob Marley, highlighting some important events in his life and giving examples of some of his most recognised songs.

8.12 CHINESE MUSIC

Chinese music is often based on the pentatonic scale. This is a scale based around 5 notes, commonly the 5 black notes on a keyboard, or C – D – E – G – A. For this reason, music which uses the pentatonic scale can allude to 'sounding' like traditional Eastern music.

8.12.1 Listening activities
Activity: Butterfly Lovers Erhu Concert posted by Welchang [1 Oct. 2013] https://youtu.be/tu5XohUR3Pg
Watch this concert which features a Chinese orchestra and note the differences between traditional Western instruments and Eastern instruments. The solo instrument is called an Erhu.

In China instruments are traditionally divided into categories based on what material they are made of: silk, skin, bamboo, gourd, wood, earth/clay, metal and stone.

8.12.2 Improvisation

Pentatonic scale. If you are using keyboards an easy pentatonic scale to use is all five black notes. Explore how to create melodies by added rhythms and deciding a pattern in which to play some of the notes. How is repetition being used? Students could have a musical conversation by taking it in turns to ask and answer musical questions.

8.12.3 Composition

Activity 1: Pentatonic composition in ABA structure

Split the class into 12 small groups and assign a Chinese zodiac animal. Each group must compose a piece of music, or write some lyrics, to illustrate the character of the animal they have been chosen. Pupils can choose to write song lyrics with verses about the Chinese Zodiac signs/animals.

Activity 1: Compose music for a Chinese New Year celebration

Combine both Western and Eastern elements of music to compose a celebration song for a Chinese New Year celebration. Watch videos of the human Chinese dragon and try to match the style of music with the dragon dance.

8.13 JAPANESE MUSIC

8.13.1 Listening

Activity: Japanese Taiko drumming

Watch this performance of Japanese Taiko drumming. Discuss how the drummers use their physicality to play the drums. Do the pupils think this is an effective way of playing the Taiko drums? Why?

YouTube – Kodo – 'O-Daiko' – HD (Japanese drummers – Taiko- tambours geants Japon) posted by AgoravoxFrance [29 Mar. 2011] https://youtu.be/C7HL5wYqAbU

8.13.2 Research
Activity 1
Music in Japan has a rich history and takes many different forms. Research some of the following genre of Japanese music and find pieces of music on YouTube to teach others about the key musical features:
- Buddhist chanting
- Taiko drumming
- Okinawa folk
- Shakuhachi music
- J-Pop
- Happy End – folk rock group
- Pyg – supergroup
- Babymetal – heavy metal

Activity 2
Find out about Koji Kondo – the sound manager for Nintendo. What tracks is he famous for composing? What other Japanese computer game music composers are there?

Activity 3
Music festivals in Japan have become more popular, for example the Fuji Rock Festival. Find out more about the music festivals in Japan and what styles of music are celebrated. Many famous Western rock bands have filmed music videos in Japan, can you research which songs this might include?

8.14 INDIAN MUSIC

India has one of the oldest civilisations in the world and there is historical evidence placing India as one of the oldest cultures at 3000 BC. India is still a very religious and spiritual country. This is reflected in the nature of the Indian classical music tradition which is built around Raga and Tala. Bhangra is traditional folk music from North India and can be recognisable from the rhythms played on Dhol drums. It has been fused with many other musical styles – house, hip-hop, disco, swing, reggae and drum 'n' bass – and enjoys popularity all over the world. The Bollywood industry generates a wealth of songs and music from its extensive repertoire of musicals.

8.14.1 Listening activities

Raga can be very relaxing to listen to and so it is a good idea to let the students get into a relaxed position, with heads on arms, or lying on the ground. Without any distractions pupils can then listen with more focus and appreciate the transcendental nature of the raga.

Activity 1: Traditional Indian classical raga

Ravi Shankar (1968) 'Dadra' from *The Sounds of India.* Columbia Records

- What term is given to the long-held note in the background? (*Drone*)
- What instrument is being played? (*Sitar*)
- What are the names of the drums that come in? (*Tabla*)
- Does the melodic part sound pre-composed or improvised? (*Improvised*)

The raga can last anything between 10 minutes up to 1 hour and uses a clear structure of different sections of music that get faster as the music progresses.

Activity 2: Bhangra

'Mundian To Bach Ke' (Panjabi MC and the Band Labh Janjua, 2003)

- Does the opening instrument sound British or Indian? (*Indian sitar playing a riff*)
- How many notes does the bass guitar play? (2)
- What type of drums are playing? (*Electric drum machine, then dhol drums*)
- Does it sound improvised? (*No, it sounds pre-composed*)

Nitin Sawhney

Nitin's music is an eclectic fusion of many different western and eastern music styles. His album *Beyond Skin* (1999) is based on the political events of India testing nuclear bombs. Describe the main British and Asian components of the following two songs:

- 'Nadia' – (Indian style singing, Indian language, westernised synthesiser chords, drum and bass rhythm part)
- 'The Conference' – (tabla drumming, call and response vocals, change in metres)

8.14.2 Singing

As a teaching resource the following book contains many accessible songs for playing with a piano or CD in the classroom: *Bollywood – Piano Favourites*, Music transcribed and arranged by O.L. Bukxari.

8.14.3 Improvisation
Activity: Raga

Use the app ThumbJam on an iPad to explore a variety of raga scales. When you have selected one develop an improvisation making sure to start on the tonic note, then slowly increasingly play the notes in the scale, always making sure to play the tonic note at the end of each phrase (musical sentence). Add a second iPad to play the drone notes to give the piece a more authentic feel.

Activity: Structure and tempo in ragas

Indian ragas are broken down into sections, which gradually throughout the improvisation increase in speed. Often there is no pulse at all in the introduction, then the soloist improvises with a pulse and more rhythm, then in the next section the tabla drums enter. The further sections increase the speed until the final notes played are energetic and virtuosic. Use this structure to develop an improvisation on ThumbJam. Add pre-composed beats underneath (from an app like LaunchPad) to create a fusion style improvisation.

8.14.4 Composition
Activity: Tala

Rhythm is an essential ingredient in all music. Rhythms in Indian music are organised by having a basic beat or pulse, which is divided up and grouped in a particular way. This is then played on a Tabla drum in cycles while a melodic instrument improvises over the top.

This tala is made up of 16 beats, which are then divided into groups of 4, so we can say it has a basic 4 metre:

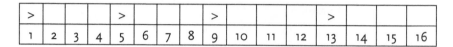

>				>				>				>			
1	2	3	4	5	6	7	8	9	10	11	12	13	14	15	16

Here are the same beats divided into different accentuations, in this case 3 + 6 + 7 (3,4), so the metre is more complex:

>		>						>			>				
1	2	3	4	5	6	7	8	9	10	11	12	13	14	15	16

Below are some more examples:

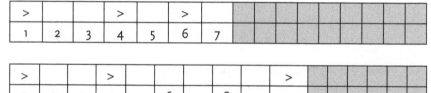

>			>		>	
1	2	3	4	5	6	7

>			>					>	
1	2	3	4	5	6	7	8	9	10

>			>		
1	2	3	4	5	6

Try composing your own talas using blank grids.

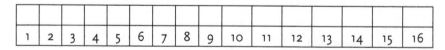

1	2	3	4	5	6	7	8	9	10	11	12	13	14	15	16

Then try layering different talas over the top of each other and see what kind of patterns you can come up with – although remember to play at the same speed as everyone else!

8.15 INDONESIAN MUSIC

Gamelan music is a style of music from the Indonesian islands of Bali and Java, situated in the Indian Ocean. The word 'gamelan' originates from the Javanese word 'gamel', meaning to hammer or strike. The instruments in a gamelan orchestra consist of percussion made from bronze and includes gongs, metallophones, xylophones, cymbals, drums and flutes. Gamelan music accompanies many traditional events in Indonesia and is also typically associated with shadow puppet plays. Gamelan is considered sacred music and out of respect musicians remove their shoes before sitting on the floor to play. They do not step over instruments as it is considered disrespectful to the spirits. It is played in groups, with no opportunities for solos and therefore showing off.

Gamelan music uses two types of scale – the slendro, a five-note scale, and the pelog, a seven-note scale. The note names are:

- slendro – pannunggal, gulu, dada, lima and enam
- pélog – bem, gulu, dhada, papat, lima, nem, barang

8.15.1 Listening
Activity 1: 'Udan Mas' ('Golden Rain'), a well-known Javanese gamelan song
- What function do the long low gong notes serve? (*Pause, separate sections*)
- Does the tempo stay the same, or change? (*Gets faster*)
- Does the melodic part have one note, or added harmonies? (*Added harmonies*)

Activity 2: 'The Madness of the Night and the Woven Stars' (Feliz Anne R. Macahis)
Watch this piece of performance theatre that includes various gamelan instruments and voices. Discuss what you notice.

Activity 3: 'Bangbung' (Sambasunda, 2016) – a modern gamelan fusion orchestra
Watch a live performance of 'Bangbung' on YouTube and discuss the Eastern influences and the western influences of the music.

YouTube–Sambasunda Bangbung Hideung, posted by Sambasunda Indonesia [18 Sep. 2018] https://youtu.be/OsPsxCFgdlw

Activity 4: 'Pagodes', movement 1, L.100 from *Estampes* (Claude Debussy, 1903) This piece demonstrates how the French impressionist classical composer Debussy was inspired by gamelan music:
- What solo instrument did Debussy compose this piece for? (*Piano*)
- Does the tempo stay the same, or fluctuate throughout? (*Fluctuate*)
- What scale of five notes gives the piece an Eastern feel? (*Pentatonic*)

8.15.2 Playing
Activity 1
Unless you have access to a gamelan orchestra, or alternatively xylophones, glockenspiels and hand percussion, it is tricky to emulate the same type of sound. The same techniques for playing – repetitive ostinato layered in polyphony – can be adopted for keyboard instruments, or technology.

Activity 2
iPad app – VJG app is an excellent resource for playing Gamelan music and teaches people not only about the types of instruments used, it also has a gamelan karaoke type play-along feature and several gamelan songs.

8.15.3 Composition
Activity: Create a Kecak
Kecak is a Balinese hindi dance and music drama created in Bali during the 1930s, traditionally played in villages and temples. The dance involves the group sitting in a circle and shouting out 'Chak' and other syllables, while moving their arms and bodies, creating multilayers of rhythmic and harmonic interest. The leader calls out instructions to lead the group into a new or repeated section. The Kecak is also known as the Ramayana monkey chant.

Research questions
- What is a gamelan?

- Name three instruments that can be found in a gamelan.
- What material are gamelan instruments typically made from?
- Name the two scales on which most gamelan music is based?
- Can you name any gamelan fusion songs?

8.16 AUSTRALIAN MUSIC

The didgeridoo is a wind instrument consisting of a wooden pipe between 1 and 3 metres in length. The longer the pipe the lower the sound. It is a ceremonial instrument used by indigenous aboriginals dating back up to 1500 years ago.

8.16.1 Listening
Activity: Australia – Sound of the Earth: Red Dust and Sweat (Steve Roach, 1990)
- How does the music convey the sense of Australia being a large expanse of desert? (*Big, long ethereal sounds and effects*)
- How does the music build up? (*A didgeridoo joins in; the rhythms get more prominent and energetic*)

Activity 2: 'Four Chords' (Axis of Awesome, 2011)
The Axis of Awesome are an Australian musical comedy group. They recorded a song called 'Four Chords' which covers as many songs as possible with the same chord progression:

D, A, Bm, G (E, B, C#m, A on live shows).

- Listen to the song and see how many different songs you can recognise.

8.16.2 Playing
Activity: 'Waltzing Matilda' chord sequences:
    Verse: D, A, D, A, D, G
        D, A, D, G, D, A, D
    Chorus: D, G, D, Em, A
        D, A, D, G, A, D,

8.16.3 Improvising
Activity: 'Four Chords' improvisation
Use the same chord sequence – D, A, Bm, G – from the Axis of Awesome song 'Four Chords' and create an improvisation over the top using the notes: D, E, F#, G, A, B, C#, D

8.16.4 Composing
Activity: Using the same chord sequence to play lots of songs
Use the same chord progression as the song 'Four Chords' by Axis of Awesome and see how many songs you can learn from their composition to create your own arrangement.

Useful websites

www.bandlab.com/
BandLab is a social media platform for composing music and contains resources and ideas for teachers.

www.bbc.co.uk/teach/ten-pieces
The BBC Ten Pieces has many teaching resources to support the musical learning of many classical pieces of music.

www.bbc.co.uk/bitesize
BBC Bitesize has teaching resources and ideas for key stage 1 to GCSE and post-16.

https://charanga.com/site/
Charanga is a very popular digital teaching platform with an extensive list of resources for all ages. Subscription is needed to access all resources.

https://collins.co.uk/pages/primary-music-music-express
Music Express is a subscription based website containing a variety of music resources for teachers.

www.efdss.org/efdss-education/resource-bank
The English Folk Dance and Song Society website gives access to many free teaching resources about folk music.

www.figurenotes.org/
The Figurenotes website supports teachers in learning how to use Figurenotes notation, which is an easier system of learning how to read music. This resource is especially good for young people with additional needs.

www.singup.org/
Sing Up contains numerous song resources although membership is required for full access.

https://midnightmusic.com.au/
Midnight Music is a website run by Katie Wardrobe who offers training, support and resources for music teachers using technology.

www.musicalfutures.org/resources
The Musical Futures website contains helpful 'Everyone Can Play Play-along' resources for ukulele and chair drumming, as well as many more resources for teachers to develop student-led learning approaches.

www.soundtrap.com/
Soundtrap enables people to make music online and is widely used in schools to help young people develop composition skills.

www.tes.com/teaching-resources
The TES (Times Education Supplement) website contains many teaching materials for primary and secondary.